WHAT
CUSTOMERS
CRAVE

WHAT CUSTOMERS
CRAVE

HOW TO CREATE RELEVANT AND MEMORABLE
EXPERIENCES AT EVERY TOUCHPOINT

NICHOLAS J. WEBB

HarperCollins
Leadership

An Imprint of HarperCollins

Published by HarperCollins Leadership, an imprint of HarperCollins Focus LLC.

Any internet addresses, phone numbers, or company or product information
printed in this book are offered as a resource and are not intended in any way to
be or to imply an endorsement by HarperCollins Leadership, nor does Harper-
Collins Leadership vouch for the existence, content, or services of these sites,
phone numbers, companies, or products beyond the life of this book.

ISBN 978-0-8144-3782-7 (eBook)
ISBN 978-1-4002-3582-7 (PBK)

Library of Congress Cataloging-in-Publication Data
Library of Congress Cataloging-in-Publication application has been submitted.

Printed in the United States of America
22 23 24 25 26 LSC 10 9 8 7 6 5 4 3 2 1

―――――――――――

I would like to dedicate this book
to my amazing family:

My wife, Michelle;
our daughters, Taylor, Madison, and Paige;
and our son, Chase.

―――――――――――

CONTENTS

CONTENTS

ACKNOWLEDGMENTS

I would like to acknowledge all of my learned colleagues in the customer experience ecosystem for all that you have taught me.

I would like to thank Dr. Ray Power, Matti Palo, MD, and my team at Learnlogic and Leaderlogic.

PART ONE

WHAT YOU NEED TO KNOW ABOUT THE CUSTOMER EXPERIENCE

In *What Customers Crave*, I focus on the current landscape of customer service—in particular, why it's so devastatingly different from what it was in the pre-connected economy age. In today's hyper-connected, hyper-competitive business world, old ways of providing customer service are failing.

As we explore this phenomenon, you will discover how power has shifted, where it now resides, and what you need to do to take advantage of this new paradigm. You will learn to identify your customers by type, rather than through traditional market segmentation. As a business owner, I don't care about classical market segmentation. I don't care what my customers' skin color is or whether they shop at Tiffany or Walmart. What I do care deeply about, to the depths of my marketing soul, is what they **love** and what they **hate**. In *What Customers Crave*, my emphasis is on helping you truly understand your customer types by showing you how to identify what they love and what they hate. These insights will allow you to create exceptional experiences for all of your customer types, across all touchpoints, and all channels—digital and non-digital.

I'll be discussing—and asking you to really lean into—insights and tools that will help you embrace our digital world. I will show you how to delight your customers and how to begin creating experiences for them—experiences that will turn them into social media mavens on your behalf.

What I'm asking from you in return is to lean into this information and be open to the new ideas and strategies involved because it's worth it—plain and simple. Your reward will be a more successful business, higher profits, and happier customers.

CHAPTER 1

THE ADVENT OF "EXCEPTIONAL" CUSTOMER SERVICE

Let's face it: today, most customer experience programs are a disaster.

Don't blame yourself, because it's not your fault that these programs are failing you. Most organizations were sold the promise that if they used the right software, analytic tools, and processes, they would be able to manage their customer relationships and deliver what their customers wanted—every time.

This approach sort of worked for a while. We understood our customers through segmentation and *who* the customer was—white, black, male, female, affluent, not so affluent, in their thirties, in their fifties—thinking demography was the key. We believed the voice of the customer (VoC) was the answer and that customer relationship management (CRM) tools and Net Promoter Scores (NPS) were critical for success.

The problem today is that this approach is almost always wrong. Yes, wrong. We cannot continue to apply old-fashioned models in today's hyper-linked and hyper-aggressive environment. In fact, even when an organization has built a reasonably good strategy, it virtually always fails in execution. According to some excellent research conducted for the software company Oracle, 93 percent of executives say that improving the customer experience is one of their organization's top three priorities in the next two years, and 91 percent wish their organization could be considered a customer experience leader in their industry. But many organizations are stuck in an execution chasm: 37 percent are just getting started with a formal customer experience initiative, and only 20 percent consider the state of their customer experience initiative to be advanced.[1]

A NEW BEGINNING: THE FALL OF THE CUSTOMER SERVICE–INDUSTRIAL COMPLEX

The term *military-industrial complex* came into common usage when President Dwight Eisenhower used it in his 1961 farewell address to the nation. Eisenhower used the term to warn the country of the dangerous relationship among the government, the military, and the arms industry. I have adapted it to the customer service–industrial complex, to warn businesspeople of the dangers inherent in the continued use of the canned "customer service" programs still in use today.

For nearly half a century, from the 1950s into the 1990s, customer service was easy. Its approach was authoritarian and did not directly connect with the consumer. Large organizations simply had control of the media through advertising and publicity and used one-way (simplex) communication to drive consumers to a specific service or product. In this way, they simply told consumers what their experience with a product or service was going to be like.

In contrast, an example of current success in our consumer-oriented economy is Uber, the ride-hailing car service. With traditional taxicabs, passengers had no control over what they would find when they got into a taxi. Sometimes passengers had good experiences, sometimes terrible ones. They felt they had little recourse but to accept what they got. Then Uber came along with its instant rating system, which let riders know exactly what other passengers had experienced with a particular driver. By the same token, the drivers could rate the passengers. In this way, both passengers and drivers could choose not to do business with people who had a reputation for obnoxious behavior.

In the old customer service–industrial complex environment, consumers were practically blind to their choices. Their social connections were limited (when compared to today), so they had no real way of determining the quality or value of a product or service. With few or no other options, they simply got what companies dealt to them. Purveyors of electronics, sellers of packaged consumer goods, hotels, airlines, and others were all experienced bullies, and there was little the consumer could do about it. This continued for decades . . . until the internet arrived.

To be fair, the customer service–industrial complex began with good intentions. Companies genuinely wanted to get closer to their market as they realized this was the path to more sales. The problem arose because they tried to create assembly-line techniques in the customer service process. In their attempt to drive efficiency and reduce costs, they looked inward—at what worked for them—and became self-focused, not customer-focused.

For this reason, most CRM systems are designed to help companies sell more products or services to customers. They're concerned with identifying profitable and not-profitable customers and using this knowledge to find ways to allocate resources. Information about consumer behavior and purchasing habits is pooled into spreadsheets, and businesses create grand marketing and customer engagement plans based on that data. The problem is that no one along the way actually gets to know what I call the Soul of the Customer˚. No one stops to identify customer types and what people really love and what they really hate. As a result, at best these systems are a waste of time and painful, and at worst counterproductive and destructive.

Can you use CRM to deliver better customer experiences while meeting your enterprise goals? Yes. But I find that most organizations use the systems from the perspective of a customer experience bully rather than that of a *disruptive innovator* looking to pioneer exceptional experiences across a customer journey.

Disruptive innovators identify weaknesses in competitive customer experiences (i.e., in old-school customer service), and then use the systems, methods, and tools of the enterprise innovator to create exceptional consumer value. In this book, I will show you how to do this.

Pablo Picasso, one of the most famous and influential artists in the twentieth century, said, "Every act of creation is first an act of destruction." He was a disruptive innovator. In order to completely change the way in which painting was done, he had to destroy the way in which people looked at art. Picasso might have done well in today's business world. This is far different from the incremental innovator, *who really doesn't destroy anything but only adds or subtracts a little bit.*

THE RISE OF THE INTERNET AND
THE BIRTH OF CUSTOMER CONNECTIVITY

In the early 2000s, the internet increased in influence and became widely available to consumers, causing an irreversible shift. Connection points, such as Yelp and Amazon, sprung up where people could rate their experiences and express their opinions about the quality of products and services. No longer did companies get to solely prescribe an experience in a way that best suited their purposes.

The consumer began to take control. The power shifted and customer service would never be the same. Rating systems that cataloged what to buy and what to avoid sprouted, and blogs that exposed bad experiences and harmful company practices popped up.

In other words, *connection architecture*—the ability to digitally link anything to anything—emerged, and it is having a tremendous impact on the success of companies of all sizes. Nest, for example, is a technology that monitors home energy usage. Based on this information, homeowners can modify their behavior and save money on their electric bills. Netflix's connection architecture destroyed Blockbuster by allowing users to receive movies and TV shows in their homes via the internet for only a small monthly charge, with no late fees and no trips to brick-and-mortar stores.

Question: *How many completely self-serving, internally, and operationally focused companies do you want to do business with?*

Answer: *None.*

CUSTOMER CONNECTIVITY IN TODAY'S HYPER-CONNECTED ECONOMY

A few decades ago, most of us didn't even have email. Smartphones were relegated to sci-fi shows. Notebooks? Only the paper kind. Laptops? Heavy, expensive, and relatively rare.

Today, we have digital ubiquity. The spread of mobile technology is so pervasive that it's rare that a potential customer is not digitally connected. Customers now have unlimited options; they can buy anything, anywhere, anytime, and they can choose from a wide range of prices and quality. Perhaps even more important, they can buy, sell, praise, or condemn with a few clicks of the mouse or taps with a finger.

Rather than stick our heads in the sand and pretend consumers don't have this power, we can instead embrace it by creating exceptional customer experiences that rise above what a customer "expects" and that demonstrate a deep understanding of their deepest loves and hates. Such experiences are so remarkable that they lead to our customers doing much of our marketing for us. To create these experiences, we have to truly understand the hearts and minds of our customers—in other words, what they love and what they hate.

Word of warning: I will drone on about this ad nauseam because it's the most important thing you can do in your business today.

IDENTIFYING YOUR CUSTOMER: CUSTOMER TYPES VS. SEGMENTATION

Given the world we live in, we can no longer understand our customers simply by grouping them based on their age, ethnicity, economic status, gender, and geography. This gets you nowhere on a good day and can bankrupt you on a bad one.

To help understand the difference between customer types and segmentation, think back to high school. In all likelihood, your high school senior class was comprised of one hundred or so kids who were seventeen or eighteen years old, and who lived in the same town. So, based on that market demographic, they should all have been marketed to in roughly the same way, right?

Wrong.

If you look at a typical high school lunchroom, you'll see it's divided into cliques, and it's the equivalent of social suicide to sit at the wrong clique's table. Theories abound that, even as adults, we're still scarred by high school social disasters!

High school cliques are architected based on what those kids hate and what they love. If you're into Java and Python and C++, then you're most likely at the geek table with your new Mac. If you idolize LeBron James, are on the team, and know the stats of your favorite NBA stars, no way are you going to sit with the geeks. You're with the jocks. Cheerleaders hang with the theater kids? I don't think so.

These groups don't evaporate when we graduate. They are with us for the rest of our lives. Sure, they may change as we age, find careers, and discover different interests, and we might even find some overlap with other types. But we still love certain things and hate others.

In order to create exceptional experiences, we as businesspeople first have to understand consumers better and then deliver relevant experiences to specific customer types. Once we truly understand the customer types within our specific business, we can begin to innovate exceptional customer experiences to each of those types, throughout their entire journey, using both digital and non-digital channels.

These cliques—or segments—can be defined as customer types. And customer types can be defined by two extremely simple concepts:

1. *What customers love*

2. *What customers hate*

That's all? Yep.

LEANING IN:
THE NEW CUSTOMER EXPERIENCE

People in the overwhelming majority of organizations believe they already deliver exceptional customer service. However, when their customers are interviewed about the quality of their service, it turns out that this isn't so. The overwhelming majority of customers believes companies are *not* delivering exceptional service.[2] So what's causing this big disconnect?

Most companies haven't transitioned from their customer service–industrial service complex past to today's connected world. They're still stuck in the old ways, the old mindsets, of customer service. They're still *internally* focused on profit rather than *externally* focused on the only thing that matters—the customers and *what they love* and *what they hate*. You must lean into the new customer experience to succeed.

THREE SIMPLE PRINCIPLES FOR CREATING EXCEPTIONAL CUSTOMER SERVICE

Success today comes from three principles that *What Customers Crave* embodies. Success isn't about some complex calculus algorithm plastered on a spreadsheet and regurgitated in a customer service training seminar. Instead, success is derived from these three principles:

1. **Understand** your customers not through their market demographics but from the perspective of what they truly love and hate.

2. **Invent** exceptional human experiences across all five touchpoints (defined later in this chapter): the pre-touch, first-touch, core-touch, last-touch, and in-touch.

3. **Express** these exceptional experiences via digital and non-digital means.

That's it. The secret sauce. It's not rocket science after all.

THREE SHIFTS IN WHAT YOUR CUSTOMERS CRAVE

What Customers Crave expresses and embraces three power shifts in customer experience: the innovation shift, the customer shift, and the connection shift. These shifts will determine your business's future. They represent the difference between the failure of the customer service–industrial complex mindset and the success you will achieve as you accept the power of the consumer and experience the wonders they can achieve for you when you provide them with exceptional experiences.

I want to emphasize that these three power shifts occur across all your customer touchpoints. It's not a push-this-button fix. Rather, you must incorporate these shifts across the entire customer experience, for all your customer types, using digital and non-digital channels.

Now, let's move on to examining the three power shifts and their implications for your business.

The Innovation Shift

In the days of the customer service–industrial complex, the best organizations in the world invented products, which they sold for a profit. They told the customer what type of experience they were going to have and went on their merry way.

The innovation shift—the creation of all kinds of products and services serving every imaginable purpose—was the culmination of today's extreme competition, where we have reached value/price saturation. As a result, successful companies now use disruptive innovation to create incredible human experiences. Uber is a perfect illustration of disruptive innovation: Uber didn't come out with a new kind of motor vehicle, but forever changed the way we use hired transportation. Likewise, Netflix broke the barrier to viewing movies at home by creating a new delivery system based on a monthly subscription fee and no other charges.

So, while businesses used to invent bright, shiny objects, successful enterprises in the future will use innovation to invent new and exquisite human experiences. This shift is huge, yet most organizations don't yet view innovation as a core competency. Those that do are winners. It's as simple as that.

The Customer Shift

Customers today have virtually unlimited options for purchasing a product or service. They can sit in a commuter train, a Starbucks, or anywhere with an internet connection and do their holiday shopping, buy a car on Carvana, or search for the latest iPhone app.

More important, with a few clicks they can vet your business and determine if they want to be your customer or not—all while they go about their daily routine.

The customer power shift is critical. It means that control has moved from the business to the customer. There's no place to hide if you deliver a lousy product and/or sloppy service. You will be vetted by customers, and that information will be shared throughout cyberspace.

On the other hand, if you're good, there is no better way to build your business. If you wrap your arms around this power shift, develop a partnership with your customers, and see them as the key to your successful business (which they inevitably are), they will look after you. They will announce your wonderfulness on every avenue of social media, and they will prime the way for you to get future customers as others Google, Yelp, or otherwise search your reputation.

Amazon is the ideal company to illustrate this point. It fully understands what customers want and what they hate, and delivers on it every time. In fact, Amazon is the founding father of the customer shift. It created *über*-ease of shopping and a dynamic customer-based rating system that allows for almost risk-free shopping.

The Connection Shift

Every one of your customers is connected during the majority of their waking hours. The extent to which this is true is actually staggering. In 2013, Google partnered with Nielsen to study more than six thousand mobile searches and their results. Here is some of what they uncovered:

- On average, each mobile search triggered two follow-up actions.

- Fifty-five percent of conversions (in-store, online, or by phone) happened within the hour.

- Seventy-three percent of mobile searches resulted in additional actions and conversions.

- Of all the searches studied, almost 50 percent were "goal oriented and conducted to help make a decision."[3]

In the process, Google coined new terms: "mobile moments" and "micro-moments."

To quote from Google's website: "Mobile has forever changed what we expect of brands. It's fractured the consumer journey into hundreds of real-time, intent-driven micro-moments. Each is a critical opportunity for brands to shape our decisions and preferences."[4]

In short, chances are your business is being Googled right now. Potential customers are checking out your online reputation to see if you're worth doing business with. The power is now in their hands. However, innovation and providing exceptional customer experiences are in your hands. Figure 1-1 illustrates the various ways in which everything is connected to everything else in our hyper-connected world.

Figure 1-1. Hyper-connectivity today.

THE BOTTOM LINE

What's most important to remember is that you must take the time and make the effort to understand what customer types your business serves, and then learn what those types love and what they hate. It's that simple—and it's that hard.

It takes time and effort to get out of the office, to hang out with your customers, to spend a week being one of your customers, and to experience what they experience. But if you do, you will know where your innovation needs to happen.

The benefit in today's business landscape is priceless. In fact, if you don't do this, you will fail—it's only a matter of when.

The *reality distortion field* (RDF) was initially used to describe Steve Jobs's charisma and its effect on the development of the Macintosh computer. Now the term is employed to describe how the charm and passion of a leader can be used to distort the scale and difficulty of a business project. I'm going to hijack the term to give you a word of warning: I believe that most organizations live in a reality distortion field. They are delusional in that they assume that if they deliver customer service at one or two touchpoints, they're good enough to compete favorably in the hyper-connected, hyper-competitive economy. They are wrong. One gap in exceptional service at any touchpoint and your business is toast.

So, once you've gained that carefully gleaned knowledge of your customers, then apply it across their entire journey with your business, and do it digitally and non-digitally across *all* touchpoints. You will stand out so far from your competitors that you wouldn't be able to see them even if you looked back.

CREATE THE PERFECT CUSTOMER EXPERIENCE: FOUR PILLARS OF SUCCESS

Accompanying the three power shifts are the four pillars of success needed to create the perfect customer experience. These pillars are really the centerpiece of this book. Follow them and your chances of success rise exponentially.

Using these four pillars, we treat customer service as a systemic process, not as a computer function or a training method. The culture of customer-centric innovation must permeate every aspect of your business. In this section, I'll show you how.

Design

While researching my first two books, I had the opportunity to study the best organizations in the world. What I learned was that they all looked at exceptional customer experiences as a *design* activity. This is a much different philosophy than was previously used when thinking about customer experiences.

DESIGN

Now, when you plan an experience, you think about how to please the customer. You think along the lines of "How and what am I going to create that's really customized and important to this customer type?"

So stop thinking of customer service as a best practice. Instead, think of it as a design activity where you're gaining insights to create beautiful experiences across a palette of touchpoints. If you're good at that, you win new customers and keep old ones.

Culture

Walk into any restaurant or business in your neighborhood and you can instantaneously tell if you're going to have a good experience or not. You know this by the expressions on the faces of the customer service people, by the vibe, by the tidiness or lack thereof, and even by the smell. These are all expressions of the company's culture.

CULTURE

"A man without a smiling face must not open shop."
—CHINESE PROVERB

Stakeholders want to work for an organization that has an important and meaningful mission based in goodness. You want to hire employees who want to work for a company that's mission-centric. That mission needs to be about delivering something worthwhile and important, and not just about profits. They're just a side benefit.

You attract good people by being good people. This is the culture that will make you win by having a well-articulated and well–internally branded mission of serving people in an authentic way. The more you try to make money by focusing only on money, the less money you make. The more you focus on delivering exceptional value and building a mission-centered culture, the more money you make.

Mother Teresa never set out to be famous. The Dalai Lama isn't looking to be a rock star. What they wanted was to deliver goodness, and they're revered throughout the world.

The organizations that do good for goodness's sake are the organizations that attract the best people.

Insights

I learned these lessons the hard way. After twenty-five years of wasting millions of dollars on failed innovations, I know a thing or two about the value of insights. As a serial entrepreneur and innovator, I've invented things that were dumb beyond belief. If I'd done a simple back-of-the-envelope calculation with most of them, and thereby gained insights into them, I'd never have wasted my time and money.

INSIGHTS

So, rather than working from inside our reality distortion field, to succeed, we must get real insights about what people love and what they hate. Again, if I'd just done that much, I would not have wasted millions of dollars.

Here's the most important lesson I learned from this quarter-century of innovation successes and failures:

Innovation is easy. The hard part is knowing what to innovate.

In the same vein, customer experience is easy. The hard part is knowing what customers love and hate so you can create exceptional experiences they love and come back for.

The staff of the **Harvard Business Review** *recently did a study that found that restaurants where you could see the chef preparing the food on average actually prepared better food. Chefs received instantaneous feedback in the way diners experienced their product. As a result of those insights, the chefs prepared better food.[5]*

Customer Types

Knowing your customers is no longer about segmenting them according to their ethnicity and bank account. It's about getting to know them deeply and understanding what they love and what they hate. Only when you have this knowledge can you create exceptional, relevant, and very human experiences for them.

The final battleground in customer service isn't some new training seminar. It's creating exceptional and relevant experiences across all five touchpoints. You can do this only when you deeply understand your customer types.

CUSTOMER TYPES

When Apple introduced the iPhone 6, there were four different models to choose from. The real reason for the four models was that Apple had identified four different customer types when it came to iPhone users, so a model was produced for each.

Apple is one of the most successful companies in the world. It spends millions of dollars making sure its phones meet the demands of these four customer types. While it doesn't have to cost you millions to deliver excellent products and services to your customers, identifying your customers by type and understanding their loves and hates is the key to thriving in today's business world.

THE TOUCHPOINT PUNCH

The four pillars of success must be integrated across each touchpoint of your customer's journey. In the real world, the number of relevant touchpoints varies. I once consulted for a major international luxury car manufacturer that developed a plan with 632 touchpoints! Can you imagine how impossible, moreover ineffective, it would be to try to implement a marketing plan with that many touchpoints?

Instead, I want to keep things simple. I want to give you something that's digestible and actionable, so I've broken the customer journey down into five interconnected touchpoints (as shown in Figure 1-2). They may not be profound, but they are real. Touchpoints are so vital to your success that I devote an entire chapter to each later in the book. However, I *touch* upon them here.

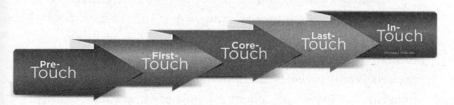

Figure 1-2. The five touchpoints.

1. The Pre-Touch Moment

This is the research phase, done digitally and non-digitally. Think back on the mobile moments and micro-moments I mentioned earlier. The digital pre-touchpoint is where your potential customers are checking you out online. They Google you and/or find reviews on Yelp, Amazon, or some other site. In other words, they're educating themselves about your online reputation *before* they actually engage with you. Underestimating the value of this touchpoint is asking for failure. Its importance will only grow over the years.

The pre-touch can also be non-digital. If you have an actual physical location, what does it look like to potential customers driving by? When customers park their cars? How about when they walk up and open the door? Are they greeted with smiles or scowls? It all adds up.

2. The First-Touch Moment

As mom always said, "First impressions last a lifetime." So it goes with the first-touch. It sets the theme for how your customer will forever perceive your product, brand, or service. If you have a bad first-touch, it's really hard to fix. Conversely, if your first-touch rocks, then you can easily build on that.

Customers checked you out in the pre-touch; here, for the first time, they actually engage with you. As with all the touchpoints, the key is to build an exceptional experience across all your customer types. Identify those types, understand what they want, then deliver it to them—exceptionally. Disney's Grand Californian Hotel & Spa is an excellent example of a first-rate pre-touch moment. As you walk in, you are greeted by the most welcoming, friendly staff. Each member of your family—from your children, to your spouse, to your parents—is treated as a special guest. It gets you in the right mood as you begin your stay in the happiest place on Earth.

3. The Core-Touch Moment

Your customer is now living with your product, brand, or service. You need to deliver the goods, day in and day out. Just gaining customers isn't enough: you have to keep reinventing great ways to serve all customer types throughout the entire relationship. Trader Joe's food stores do the core-touch perfectly. Day after day, week after week, the stores tell a new story. In the fall, they offer pumpkin spice cookies and coffee; in the spring, it's fresh vegetables and flowers. Their employees are cheerful, helpful, and apparently happy to be working there. It's Trader Joe's attention to the details that makes it so good.

4. The Last-Touch Moment

The last-touch of a particular experience is the final moment the customer has with a product or service. (Actually, there should never be a last-touch, because, ideally, you will have many more touches with all your customers.) At this touchpoint, you send your customer off with a memorable goodbye that makes them want to come back. It's a way to thank them for being with you, to tell them that you valued the experience and hope they did too.

5. The In-Touch Moment

This is how and when you stay connected with your customers after their experience with you has ended. You must approach this with an absolute commitment not to try to sell them anything, but rather to consistently and pleasantly provide them with ongoing value. You want them to willingly come back to you of their own accord, not because you're shoving some One Time Only shenanigan down their throat.

CRM software packages are often used to sell people something. They enable companies to stay in touch for the purpose of getting customers to buy something else. But this isn't what customers love; it's what they hate. Instead, deliver ongoing constant value. Let your customers know about special offers only if you know it's something they need to have.

TAKEAWAYS

Science backs up this new body of knowledge about customer service. *What Customers Crave* presents the science of how to predictably and consistently deliver exceptional customer service across all your customer types via digital and non-digital channels. We know from our experience that it works—every time.

The only commitment you have to make is a willingness to lean into the information and to accept the discomfort of learning new requirements and a new way of viewing the customer service landscape.

Albert Einstein said, "The measure of intelligence is the ability to change." This certainly holds true for the shifts in power we see today in customer service.

CHAPTER 2

BRING HOME THE BACON:
THE VALUE OF CUSTOMER TYPES

Beliefs—those things people really love and really hate—are the essence of a customer type. When you reach the point where you understand people at this emotional level, you will have discovered where your power lies. You will have discovered how to make your customers feel special and relevant in their relationship to the product or service you provide. In turn, they will remember you and give you more business, all the while referring your product or service to their friends.

This concept may seem simple and not particularly profound. You may wonder why I am even stating it, but the truth is the overwhelming majority of organizations talk about customers as if they were a monolithic demographic to whom they deliver products and services. The essence of my message in this book is that hyper-competition mandates that we do a far better job of identifying our customer types so that we can invent better and more relevant human experiences that will enable us to keep their support.

Once you identify customer types within your customer base, you will no longer attempt to provide customer service based on something as lame as simply targeting a thirty-year-old affluent Latina (for example). It's an insult to all thirty-year-old affluent Latinas to assume they have the same likes and dislikes. They might have some similarities by virtue of their age or income or ethnicity or gender, but that's not enough if you want to create exceptional and—most important—relevant customer experiences.

Identifying customer types helps you move from *what* your customers are to *who* they are. The best companies in the world understand the loves and hates of their customers. They understand the different customer types and invent a range of exceptional customer experiences across these types. As a result, they're kicking butt.

When you understand your customers by what they love and hate (their types) and not through their demographic characteristics (such as skin color and/or age), you begin to provide relevant and memorable human experiences. One of the most common mistakes organizations make when it comes to the customer experience derives from their erroneous belief that delivering what the customer wants is good enough. In the days of the customer service–industrial complex, that was fine. But in today's connected economy, where customers have more choices, we have to go above and beyond what they expect. The key to customer experience is the difference between providing what the customer expects versus what you deliver. When you go far beyond what they expect, you have given them a memorable customer experience. By doing so, you will achieve unprecedented levels of profit and growth because your customers will be talking about you.

Walk into an Apple store, and the first thing the sales representative does is find out what kind of customer you are. Are you the transactional type, who just wants an iPhone cord? Or do you want to fiddle with the latest laptop? Is price your thing, so you are looking for the most gigs for your buck? Once the rep finds out what matters to you, they send you on a relevant journey and deliver what you are looking for.

I recently spoke with a real estate agent who had gone to a car dealer to purchase a new car. In her business, specializing in luxury homes for successful baby boomers, she serves a bold clientele. What she needed more than anything in her new car was a luxurious back seat, one high enough to make it easy for her clients to get in and out of the car. Instead, the salesperson delivered his prepared speech about the engine and suspension. He not only didn't deliver what she wanted, but he didn't even hear her. Needless to say, she walked away without buying a car from him.

If you identify customer types and act upon that knowledge, you move from providing exceptional customer service to only a small percentage of your customers to providing exceptional and customer-appropriate service across an entire range of customer types and therefore to a much larger percentage of your customers.

BECOME A CUSTOMER SERVICE *STANDOUT*: TWO EASY-TO-APPLY FORMULAS

Here are two easy-to-understand formulas, which we'll be drilling down on throughout the book. The two key formulas are the Power Shift Insights Formula and the *What Customers Crave* Innovation Formula. The first formula is designed to help you learn what makes your customers tick so you can fully understand and identify your customer types. The second formula is a four-step process that allows you to invent world-class customer-driven innovations, which I call CDIs.

The Power Shift Insights Formula:
H + L = CT

Knowing what a customer **Hates** (H) and knowing what a customer **Loves** (L) equals their **Customer Type** (CT).

That's it. I told you it was simple.

Here's an example of the formula. In my town, we have a burrito restaurant called Burrito Bandito, which in my opinion makes outstanding burritos. They're so popular that they often have a long line. But even though I love their burritos, I won't go there because I hate standing in line. My wife, however, loves the burritos more than she hates standing in line, so she goes there. My wife and I are different customer types. If she loves something, she'll stand in line, while I'm the opposite.

The *What Customers Crave* Innovation Formula:
N + O + D + E = CDI

After much research, I discovered a four-step process to create customer-driven innovations (CDIs) that allows you to deliver the best experiences to your customer types. This simple formula begins with **Navigating** (N) to where the customer is, then **Observing** (O) what the customer hates and loves, and then **Designing** (D) new experiences that will amaze them. Last, you need to **Execute** (E) aggressively and be able to measure the results. Implementation of this process makes it easy for you to achieve customer experience superstardom. Figure 2-1 depicts the *What Customers Crave* Innovation Formula.

Figure 2-1. The What Customers Crave *Innovation Formula.*

THE ROLE OF MARKET SEGMENTATION

In the past, market segmentation has been a sales tool used to figure out how to sell more stuff. In both the digital and non-digital world, of course, segmentation still has a role to play. If, for example, you are appealing to a Latinx market, you probably should include information in English and Spanish on your website. If you're appealing to physicians, you might use a certain vocabulary and set of resources.

What no longer works is using this marketing methodology to try to gain insights into how to design exceptional and relevant human experiences. Understanding your customers doesn't work that way. Unfortunately, in the past we either saw customers as one broad market segment—a thirty-something affluent

Latina—and failed to dissect that segment into customer types to truly understand their different loves and hates, or we attempted to further define them but used an easy-to-characterize statistical driver that didn't really get to *who* that customer was.

Sometimes I am asked if there is overlap between segmentation and customer types. My answer is always, "Yes and no." Here's an example. A client in the funeral business learned that war veterans were a segment of his consumer base. My client had been marketing to this group just as he marketed to any other. He asked me to find out if veterans had unique characteristics and needs that he was missing when marketing to and serving this group.

My team found huge differences in what veterans were looking for compared to other customer types. For example, there were unique ways to celebrate a veteran's life as well as in what the funeral service should look like, the specific vernacular, and even in the way loss was communicated. So my client created a range of materials that spoke specifically to the veteran customer type.

AVOID A "ONE BUCKET" CUSTOMER EXPERIENCE AND MAXIMIZE CUSTOMER SATISFACTION

The best way to fail in the hyper-competitive marketplace is to attempt to deliver a one-size-fits-all customer experience. We all serve a market segment, but within our market segment there are customer types who want to engage our products and services differently based on their hates and loves.

Take Southwest Airlines, for example. In order to be profitable in the airline industry (one of the toughest and most competitive markets on the planet), you need to be able to deliver services to a large customer market, i.e., people who are flying. However, within this large market are "micro markets" representing a range of customer types.

I fly Southwest regularly as a business traveler, and the airline has designed a customer experience for just my type of passenger. By paying a bit extra for my ticket, I get to be one of the first fifteen passengers on the plane, guaranteeing me a place to stow my carry-on. As a business traveler, I cannot afford canceled flights, and Southwest's predictably on-time schedule addresses my need to show up on time for client meetings and speaking engagements. Where other airlines struggle, Southwest is rarely late.

Southwest knows that to succeed it has to reach a broader market with different needs than mine, so the airline has developed a pricing strategy to make flying affordable for everyone. Southwest is also surgical in choosing which cities it flies to and in its choice of planes to fly, which helps reduce service costs.

The airline also developed a way to accommodate travelers with disabilities. Such travelers don't have to present a doctor's note or other proof of disability. Instead, they get to board first just by saying they are disabled. It's simple, elegant, and painless. Southwest also treats young travelers like royalty. They get wings pinned on them and get to meet the captain. For many kids, it may be the most memorable experience of their young lives, and it distracts the ones who might be a bit frightened. Southwest knows its customer types and has something unique in its quiver for each.

There's much more I could say about what Southwest Airlines has done right, but for our purpose, it's important to understand that the company's success comes from first identifying its customers by type. Having done that, the company invents relevant and exceptional experiences for each and every customer type. Had Southwest gone after only frequent fliers and other more profitable customers, I doubt it would be leading the airline industry as it does.

The takeaway here is to:

- Look at your micro market.

- Identify the ranges of customer types.

- Invent perfect experiences across all these customer types.

Why the Mainstream Gurus Are Wrong

If you were to talk to the customer experience experts born from the customer service–industrial complex, they would disagree with everything I just said. They would argue that you should identify your most profitable customers and only develop experiences relevant to them.

If you're like me, though, you've got to be thinking, "Why would I eliminate any customer who delivers potential profit to my business?" You are also probably asking yourself, "Why don't I come up with a way to make those so-called 'nonprofitable customers' profitable?" If that's your train of thought, you're on the right track.

> *If we want to sell our products and services to real human beings, and if we want to make emotive, relevant connections as we deliver excellence, then we need to understand people. We need to understand who they are, not just what they are demographically.*

Here's an example from my own life. You probably have a similar one.

I run every morning with a group of guys. We're all men in our mid-fifties, and we live in the same neighborhood in similar houses, and have similar incomes. However, one guy is politically conservative, and another is liberal. One is super-religious, and another is an atheist. One is personally very assertive, while another looks for a consensus. According to our demographic, we're all from the same one-dimensional market segment, but in reality we have very different loves and hates. If our customer service experiences were identical—based on gender, age, income, and race—it would work for a few of us, but not all. Our loves and hates are very different. But if our experiences were based on customer types where our individual loves and hates were identified, our customer service experiences would be different. Done correctly, incredible and relevant customer experiences can be delivered that appeal to different types across all five touchpoints.

Take running shoes, for example. Based on the same demographics of gender, age, socioeconomic status, and race, my running friends and I should all like the same running shoes, right? Of course not. What's more important is whether we run or walk, if we have injuries, if we are experienced or new to running, and so on. You can't use empirical data to determine what we hate and what we love because it's impossible to create exceptional experiences based on macro information. "Exceptional" means "relevant," and that's different for each of us. Religion, for example, doesn't matter when it comes to selecting the right shoes. You select shoes based on how you use those shoes. CRM data doesn't give you that information.

INNOVATION SUCCESS VS. FAILURE: A SIMPLE STRATEGY

As a management consultant and successful inventor, I've been involved in the innovation space for more than a quarter of a century. After wasting millions of dollars developing awkward and irrelevant products for consumers (as I've mentioned previously), I finally learned something that was literally life-changing:

"Inventing is EASY . . . Knowing what to invent is really HARD."

I learned from researching the best innovators that they're extremely judicious in choosing what they want to invent. Most people invent customer products and technology by making assumptions about a need or problem, and then they invent the item based on those assumptions. What they're missing are real insights about what the customer hates and loves. Consider that of the thousands of patents issued for new products and technology over time, only 2 percent are successful. The technology might be great, but the products are irrelevant to the customer.

Other people create great products based on their potential clients' loves, but they don't check in with those end users soon enough to prevent disasters. For example, Crayola is a fabulous company. It's really well run and delivers great products. I can't say enough good things about Crayola. However, even the best companies don't always hit home runs. In the early 1990s, Crayola came up with a way to make colored bubbles. Conceptually, the idea was sound: Kids love blowing bubbles and love colors. Put these two together and you create this great experience for kids, right? It was a disaster. Turns out those colorful bubbles stained everything they landed on—carpets, curtains, tiny faces, you name it. Although they're still on the market, the social media ratings are terrible. Crayola would have avoided the staining colored bubbles had it tested the product on parents and kids. Crayola is one of the best brands in the world, but when you innovate, mistakes can happen to any of us.

As I've said, all great innovations come from understanding what customers love and what they hate. You must experience what your customers experience. The more you know, the more you can create relevant experiences.

So here's the obvious question: How do you know what to invent? The answer is simple: identify your range of customers by the things they emotionally love and hate. Crayola knew what *kids* love; they're experts. Unfortunately, this time the company delivered a fractional experience by not experiencing what the kids' *parents* hated.

Take a look at the consumer packaged goods industry. Great companies like Procter & Gamble are experts at knowing what consumers love and hate so they can create relevant, inexpensive, and effective products. They created complete industrial categories within the consumer packaged goods sphere to address those loves and hates. They are really good at going from inconvenient to convenient.

Consumers hate cleaning toilets, so the Clorox Company came up with a range of toilet cleaners based on customer types, because not everyone hates cleaning toilets for the same reason. For example, some consumers were interested in a toilet that felt sterile, so P&G devised products with high germ kill rates. Other consumers were more concerned about odor, so a range of products emerged to address that preference. Still others hated physically cleaning the toilet, so no-touch solutions like the Clorox ToiletWand were created to insulate them.

The best innovations and best human experiences are created based on exceptionally good consumer insights. As you will discover, when we identify a way to serve one customer type, we typically provide a new benefit for all customers.

VALUE STACKING: THE SECRET WEAPON FOR CUSTOMER EXPERIENCE SUCCESS

When we get very granular about what a range of customer types hates and loves, layering occurs. As we invent better experiences, we stack the value through different customer types—what works for one customer type also works for other customer types—and that's how we get to perfect human experiences.

If a fast-food restaurant creates a great burger but has a long line, it is able to sell burgers only to customers who love burgers and don't hate long lines. The options are to create a shorter line by hiring more staff or to design a more efficient system for producing a great burger. The best organizations, however, do both. They learn what customers hate and what customers love across a well-defined range of identifiable customer types.

KNOW YOUR CUSTOMER TYPES: CREATE AN IMPACTFUL MESSAGE

I have a full speaking schedule every year. When I get up onstage, I'm not worried about what I'm supposed to be talking about. Instead, I'm thinking about the people in front of me in the seats. It took me a long time to realize that the words themselves don't matter. The only thing that matters is the people in the seats and how I can make my talk reach them in a way that truly has meaning. Every person in that room—not just some of them—needs to be moved by my message in a way that fulfills them intellectually and emotionally.

I learned this the hard way a few years ago when I gave a talk for physicians and caregivers at a large cancer hospital. In planning it, I assumed the audience wanted to hear a somber story about overcoming cancer. I had no evidence for this; I just assumed it. So I delivered deep, heartfelt content that was as serious as, well, cancer. And it bombed.

The next speaker delivered absolutely no content, but he made the audience laugh. He delivered humor and was rated the event's top speaker. I, on the other hand, was rated near the bottom.

I hadn't taken the time to really understand who the audience was and what they wanted from me. They knew all about the horrors of cancer, of course; they lived with it every day! What they wanted was to *laugh*. Had I made the investment in time and energy to type my audience, I would have been a success because I can make people laugh. This is a mistake I've never made again. Today, I'm very careful about learning who my audience is and what they want from me, and I devote all the energy and time necessary to it because in the end that's what matters.

The foundation of an exceptional human experience is making sure that what you design is relevant.

If I'm looking for the latest and most powerful smartphone but the salesperson shows me the cheapest and smallest model, that's not going to be a relevant experience for me. If it's not, it's not going to resonate for me.

Relevance is the prerequisite for exceptional.

Apple is excellent at building an exceptional consumer experience journey. The company politely probes to find out what a customer loves or hates, and then invents and communicates a relevant experience for that particular customer type.

When an experience is relevant, the exceptional part comes automatically. Relevance is the cornerstone of an exceptional human experience.

YOUR SELLERS ARE ALSO YOUR CUSTOMERS, AND THEY ARE NOT ALL ALIKE

I discovered an excellent example of the importance of understanding who your customers truly are while working for the luxury automobile manufacturer I mentioned in Chapter 1—the one with 632 touchpoints. While in the discovery process, we unearthed an important layer of customer types.

This is an enormous company with a household name, and with half a million or so employees worldwide. The company executives spend tens of millions of dollars on trendy analytics. However, despite all the data pooling and Excel spreadsheets, they missed a very basic yet tremendously important concept: they hadn't thought to analyze their *dealer* types. They weren't communicating in effective and relevant ways to the individuals who were selling their cars. Instead, there were simply "big dealerships" and "small dealerships." This was a serious mistake.

When we interviewed the individual dealers and began learning what they loved and hated, we found three distinct dealer customer types: the Evangelist, the Pragmatist, and the Pessimist. These three highly relevant types were dispersed pretty evenly between big and small dealerships. It quickly became obvious that the *size* of the dealership didn't matter nearly as much as the *type*.

> *There may be more than one layer of customer types in a company. In this case, for example, there may be dealers, suppliers, senior managers, middle managers, low-level managers, wholesalers, retailers, and so on.*

The Evangelist customer types loved everything about the car brand. They drove it, they wore the logo on their shirts and jackets, they bought their spouse brand trinkets for Christmas, and they let everyone in the neighborhood know what they did for a living and how much they loved it. They were fervent brand ambassadors. They embraced whatever the marketing arm pushed out.

The Pragmatists were a different sort altogether. These dealers were businesspeople who saw the car brand as an object on the shelf. The Pragmatists' reason for working at this company was to transmute the physical car into a profit. That was it. Done. The Pragmatists liked the brand to the extent that it sold well, that the margins were good, and that the company was spending money to help drive sales. Their interest was practical and operational. If the brand made them money, they liked it. If it didn't make them money, they didn't like it. They weren't in any way emotional about it. They could have just as easily sold for another car company.

The Pessimists were the third and biggest dealer type. These individuals saw the car manufacturer as a bully who was always pushing them to sell more cars, to have more prominent logos, to spend more money on local advertising, and to do this and that. The Pessimists thought the company had unrealistically high expectations of them and provided little support to back them up. If customers didn't come in and spend their money, the Pessimists would leave and join another company.

The one hard and fast rule about customer types is . . . there is NO hard and fast rule.

No one set of customer types fits across all companies. So, throughout this book, I'll show you how to build out new types specific to your product, service, and market.

The solution is to roll up your sleeves and go deep. It takes time and energy. Identifying customer types requires strategic listening, contact point innovation, and understanding the Soul of the Customer (all discussed later in this book). Through this process, you learn how to design exceptional and relevant human experiences across the customer journey.

Previously, the company had communicated with and treated each dealer type identically. After my team and I explained the different dealer types and showed management what each loved and hated, they understood that the company needed three different approaches, not one, to reach each of them. What would work for an Evangelist would fall flat or worse with a Pessimist. Until then, the company had approached its dealers in a one-dimensional way with marketing, company programs, and even financial incentives. The company was wasting tens, if not hundreds, of millions of dollars in spillage using this inaccurate and damaging dealership communication.

We then helped the company build three different messaging programs that would speak to each dealer type in a relevant way:

- The Evangelists loved the brand. They wanted to learn all they could about the new models, the features they could share, and the ways they could help their customers become evangelists too. Their entire universe was their love of the brand and their desire to share its benefits.

- The Pragmatists only wanted to understand the math: how the product related to their customers and what the financial upsides and downsides were. They needed the details about return options, any mechanical issues that had come up, and other practical information.

- The Pessimists, on the other hand, needed evidence. They wanted the company to prove its programs wouldn't hurt them and would ultimately be beneficial. They wanted statistics and data to support everything.

By truly understanding what each type loved and hated, we were able to invent exceptional and relevant experiences for each group.

WHERE TO BEGIN:
HOW TO UNCOVER YOUR COMPANY'S CUSTOMER TYPES

To identify your customer types, you can't take a set of generic customer types, slap them onto your consumer experience strategy, and then expect to provide your customers with relevant experiences. You must begin at the beginning with your own customers.

To illustrate how to go about identifying customer types and designing relevant, exceptional consumer experiences across various touchpoints, using both digital and non-digital channels, let's work with a fictional company—a car wash called NeoWash. The process begins with three simple steps.

Step 1:
Brainstorming Session

Ideation is a ten-dollar word for brainstorming, the process of forming images or ideas. It's a good place to begin. Start by asking yourself what commonly known attributes of the human experience might impact the customers of NeoWash. For example, you can anticipate that in a car wash some people are primarily interested in fast service, others in high quality, and still others in low cost above all other traits.

Once you have come up with a range of theoretical customer types, you must test and refine these types using two things:

1. Digital analytics—tools used to assess qualitative and quantitative online data about your current and potential customers.

2. Contact point innovation—inventing at the point at which the experience is being delivered rather than in the boardroom or laboratory, far away from where customers actually experience the service or product.

In other words, bring your team to the car wash's parking lot and start by seeing how the cars enter and exit.

I remember learning about an architect who built amazing buildings and then planted grass all around them so that there were no obvious paths leading to the entrances and exits. Weeks later, he simply created concrete pathways on the mashed-down trails that had been organically made by people walking to the doors. This is contact point innovation.

You then refine these types as they engage in the five contact points across your company. The net benefit is that the new experiences you invent across each contact point and customer type will be relevant across your entire range of types.

If your customers are transactional and all they want to do is get in and buy what they came for, then make that experience as amazing as possible.

If your customers are experiential, and they want to fiddle with the new gadgets and gawk at the amazing displays, then provide that for them.

If price is their issue, show them what's on sale or how to save money by downsizing the product.

Different customer types want different things. Try your best to fulfill their expectations.

As I've already mentioned, I hate waiting. My wife, being an amiable customer type, can wait for hours for what she wants. You could type me as an impatient, detail-oriented, customer-experience snob; my wife would be the opposite type. In either case, if the loves and hates are shared, that type could also include a thirty-something Latina, a twenty-something rapper, and a low-income retired schoolteacher. If you design an exceptional and relevant experience, each of us will respond to it, although our outward demographics are very different.

Step 2:
Listening Posts and Contact Point Innovation

The next step is to refine your customer types through listening posts and contact point innovation, both critical in designing the overall customer journey. A listening post literally means having someone listening to your customers. This can be accomplished in different ways—for example, physically, as in standing in line with them, or digitally.

Contact point innovation helps you:

- *Clarify and refine your customer types.*

- *Begin to design exceptional human experiences for these customer types across the range of five contact points via digital and non-digital channels.*

Contact point innovation means experiencing what your customers experience at each of the five consumer contact points. You do this by setting up listening posts at each point through both digital and non-digital channels.

At NeoWash, you could begin by experiencing the pre-touch contact point, which could be either digital or non-digital. This is the very first time the potential customer has contact with your business.

Digitally, you might Google "best car washes" in your town and see what came up. Let's say Google shows seven ratings for NeoWash with an average of 3 out of a possible 5. In the online rating world, this is bad news. You might then go over to Yelp and see five ratings with an average of 2 out of 5. Confirmation of bad news! Then, you could read the comments to find out what people hate about NeoWash. Go to other bulletin boards and blogs, as many as you can find, to learn why people think the car wash sucks. Most important, by doing this, you are experiencing firsthand the digital pre-touch contact point.

Not everyone's first contact with NeoWash will be digital. An eight-five-year-old might not have the same first experience, because he might not be as digitally savvy. He might not even know how to access these influential social networks. Instead, he might drive past your car wash and look at it. This is the first non-digital contact. What does your car wash look like? What first visual impression does it give? Is there a long line of cars waiting to be washed? Are the windows clean? Is the sign clear and does it look new? Are your staff wearing uniforms, or at least branded work shirts and caps?

The important takeaway here is that these first impressions are critical, and once you know what they are, you can invent new and amazing first impressions across the range of your customer types.

Step 3:
Repeat the Process:
Undergo the Entire Customer Experience

I wouldn't stop at the pre-touch experience. Each of the five touchpoints needs to be assessed from the perspective of a range of customer types. Remember, the disruptive innovator looks at the universe from the viewpoint of what she can create. She's designing new ways to create exceptional human experiences. She's going to invent ways to solve each broken touchpoint.

Therefore, your next step at NeoWash could be to sit in the car wash for days, watching, listening, and asking questions. What sort of people are coming in? What are they experiencing? By doing this, you refine what your customer types love and hate. You might also identify new types or combine types. You will be able to identify broken systems and opportunities to improve them by inventing human experiences that are more relevant for each customer type. For example, you might learn that church gets out at 11:00 AM, and that's why people show up at 11:15. Talk to your customers. Ask them where they're coming from and where they're going. Learn from them.

You also want to experience your employees' perspectives, which as we've seen is critical to excellent customer service. What do they need that they don't have? What's their day like? What do they love and hate about their work? When and how do they interact with the customers? What can you see about your employees through your disruptive innovator eyes? Employees want to deliver exceptional service, but maybe there are policies or systems in place that don't allow them to do this. Maybe they're lacking the resources that would help them get their jobs done better. Listen to them. Talk to them. See firsthand the quality they can deliver.

Through this process, you will begin to understand and dissect your customers and therefore customer types by what they love and hate about both their digital and non-digital journeys. You will then be able to identify ways to add layered value across the five touchpoints to the entire range of types. Remember that when you drill down on any individual customer type, you probably create layered value across all the other types. For example, if you increase the speed of service at the car wash by using time motion data, it would obviously please customers whose prime interest is speed. But all your customer types benefit from faster service. And when you increase the quality of the car wash for the customers who are primarily looking for that, all your customer types likewise benefit.

Identifying customer types increases your ability to gain the insights necessary to drive disruptive and breakthrough innovations. If you collapse the value of one customer type while inventing for another, then you're not finished inventing. All innovations should have a neutral or positive impact across all the other customer types.

The brainstorming session, listening posts, and contact point innovation helped me find four distinct customer types for NeoWash, as shown in Figure 2-2: Sparkly, Speedy, Thrifty, and Touching.

Figure 2-2. NeoWash's four customer types.

Sparkly

I'll call the first customer type Sparkly. This is a group of people who actually don't care what they pay. They don't even mind how long they have to wait. Their primary love is leaving with a perfectly clean car. They want quality; they hate having to wipe away missed spots and smudges. They're the ones holding up the line, pointing out imperfections to the final detailing guy.

As a disruptive innovator, you realize the quality control system at your car wash is broken. You are going to fix that broken system to please the Sparkly customer type. You are going to hire a senior citizen. What? Yes, I mean that. You put him in a bright orange quality control vest, and his only job is to do the final inspection of each car before it's released to the customer. He will be the final quality assurance person. Maybe you even put candy canes in his pocket for the kids.

> **Designing human experiences** *is a term you'll see throughout this book. When you identify customer types, you design these experiences better, because you're identifying not just* what *people are, but more important,* who *they are and how they wish to experience a range of touchpoints across digital and non-digital channels.*

Speedy

I've named the second customer type Speedy. He or she has one priority—speed, obviously. They hate waiting; they love fast service. They're busy and digitally savvy. Some days they have a good experience at the car wash, but on other days they must wait far too long and leave dissatisfied. As you identify this customer type, you also identify another broken system: reliably fast service.

Throughput analysis, or fast track methodology, has been in use for years. You can apply this same methodology to NeoWash. You can identify time inefficiencies throughout the entire process—

from onboarding a car through delivering it spotless and clean at the other end. If you get even more innovative, you could hire a NASCAR pit crew to give you their insights, and you could develop an app that would allow Speedy to book their time slot in advance.

This would completely change Speedy's relevant experience. With a reserved time slot, when they arrive, they'll drive past the other cars straight to the "Fast Track" lane, which has been designed to look like a NASCAR pit stop. Speedy now knows exactly when their car will be washed, and because it is prescheduled, it will all be done quickly and reliably.

As a by-product, because you used fast track methodologies and time motion studies to significantly increase the throughput of cars, you are able to reduce labor costs. So while you were providing a relevant experience to one customer type (Speedy), you are now able to offer lower-cost car washes to other customer types (those who are willing to wait). Chances are all your customer types will appreciate fast service at a fair price. Remember stacking values? That's exactly what this is.

Thrifty

Not surprisingly, one of your customer types is primarily cost conscious. These customers' loves and hates revolve around price, so I've called them Thrifty. For this type, do a price sensitivity analysis. Talk to customers, look at your competitors' prices, and see what you can do to become more relevant to your Thrifty customer type.

Part of the magic is that, as you helped Speedy, you might be able to help Thrifty, who might also want a faster car wash. This is the beauty of stacked innovation. As you identify ways to deliver value and relevancy to one customer, you create a by-product that allows you to deliver benefits to another customer.

In the process of using fast track methodologies and time motion efficiency analysis to help out Speedy, you reduce labor costs by increasing efficiencies. This allows you to deliver the most competitive price package to Thrifty. Undoubtedly, other customer types will appreciate this as well.

You could also look at the days and times with the slowest business and offer Thrifty a $5 discount if a wash is reserved for those times. This is a good business move for the company and great value for a type who's looking for cheaper car washes.

Touching

I call the final customer type Touching. This is the person who sees going to the car wash as an experience. It could be the stay-at-home mom or dad or a retiree wanting to get out of the house. For them, it's about the touch, the experience, and the emotive qualities. What does the car wash smell like? Sound like? Feel like? Is there a friendly person there to greet them and a place for kids to play? Is there a nice merchandise area?

As a disruptive innovator designing human experiences for Touching, you invent a sensory emotion across each contact point. You get their shoes polished and have espresso coffee and fresh croissants available in the morning. Touching loves the actual experience, so give them an exceptional one. They may not always have the time to linger, but it'll be an option.

You might even create a Clean Concierge Club. For club members who get their car washed twice a month, the espresso and croissant are free, and there is a separate area with cushy leather couches just for them. They can sign up for the club online and can accumulate points to be used on extra services.

Every time I've seen a company identify its most profitable customers and place most of its resources there, I've found that these customers were the most profitable because they were subscribing to what that company was doling out.

How about making nonprofitable customers profitable? Understand your customers across all your customer types. Walk around, be disruptive, and look at what you can create that's new and relevant by looking at what you can destroy. This is the best way to come up with disruptive ideas and turn nonprofitable customers into profitable ones.

TAKEAWAYS

Do you think you'd find these layers of value if you used only traditional market segmentation? No, you wouldn't. Identifying customer types and delivering relevant human experiences across their entire range creates exceptional, layered value. Do this throughout each contact point and via digital and non-digital channels and you truly will be designing exceptional and relevant human experiences.

To identify and understand your customer types, you must experience what your customer experiences, identify what's broken, and invent relevant new experiences both digitally and non-digitally. Remember to **Navigate** where your customer is across the customer journey. **Observe** what your customer loves and hates. **Design** better experiences across all your customer types. **Execute** the innovations that your customer loves.

You're not going to die if you get this wrong the first time. You can't even break it. What you will do is start the process of inventing an amazing range of new value you can deliver. It's a new way of looking at your customer, which creates the seed of thought for driving the next big idea.

It takes courage to look at what you're currently doing and say it's bad. It takes courage to turn what you're doing on its head and try something else. But the downside is to do the same old thing and get your butt whipped by the disruptive innovator down the road.

CHAPTER 3

THE JOURNEY TO EXCEPTIONAL CUSTOMER EXPERIENCES

Customer service is dead. Gone. Bye-bye. If you're using customer service as a way to lead your market segment—in fact, even if you're just trying to deliver good customer service—you've already lost.

Good customer service = bad customer experiences.

What? Isn't customer service what it's all about?

No. The way you "serve" a customer is only one sliver of the total customer experience. Good customer service will kill your business because most customer service initiatives are not enough to allow you to compete effectively in today's market. So not only is good customer service dead, it can be deadly.

If you're just trying to deliver what customers expect, you might as well kiss your business goodbye.

In the "good old days," those who were part of the customer service–industrial complex could bully their customers into telling them the kind of experience they wanted. For example, for years, patients who needed to see their doctor had to make an appointment at the doctor's convenience and at the doctor's location. Waiting times were notoriously bad, and people often had to sit for hours in germ-ridden waiting rooms until the doctor saw them. Now, there are programs such as Anthem's LiveHealth Online, where you can wait in the comfort of your living room, go online from your favorite device, and chat or speak to a doctor in minutes—at your convenience, at your location, and with little or no waiting time. Afterward, you can even rate your experience.

Today we have empowered and engaged consumers who express their experiences, loves, and hates using hyper-influential social media. They have an almost unlimited number of options for where and how to spend their money. It is no longer about customer service. Instead, it's about customer experiences, and those had better be exceptional and relevant ones.

In this chapter, I use a very different definition of an exceptional customer experience, because not only do most businesses not know their customer, but they also don't know what exceptional service is.

DESIGNING *EXCEPTIONAL* INTO THE CUSTOMER EXPERIENCE

There is no one set of exceptional customer experiences that will work across an entire range of companies and customer types. You must invent the experiences that fit your market, service, product, and customer types.

The good news is inventing is easy.

The bad news is it's hard to know *what* to invent.

Fortunately, the precursor to knowing what to invent is knowing *whom you're inventing for*. Once again, it comes down to customer types. When you've taken the time and energy to truly understand your customers and identified and refined their types, you will be light-years ahead of your competitors in designing exceptional and relevant human experiences. You will know what each customer type loves and hates because you will have peered into their souls.

> *Success doesn't come from just providing customer service. It's about engineering a complete customer experience that's exceptional and relevant across a range of customer types. Understand this or watch your business die in the face of today's heated competitive environment.*

WHO BENEFITS? LOOK OUT, NOT IN

So what exactly are "exceptional customer experiences"? Throughout the years, I've interviewed thousands of CEOs, middle managers, frontline service representatives, and every other level of service provider, all the way down to janitors. Each time I asked for a definition of customer service, I got either a different answer or a canned, meaningless mission statement.

The real tragedy, however, is that most of the people I interviewed who had a definition of customer service centered it on increasing profit and driving revenue. Most customer service initiatives are centered on approaches that are highly fractional (inconsistent service within a company) and highly internalized (inward looking). For example, in a company, the finance department manager's idea of customer service focuses on something to do with finance. The marketing department guru's approach has something to do with marketing. The IT department head's idea has to do with technology and support. All of these examples show how fractionalized and internalized this company's process has become: everyone views their role and success from the perspective of their individual department, not as a unified company with a unified message. What's more, they're looking in at themselves, not out at the customer.

Underlying each of these fractional and internalized views are questions like these:

- How can the company make more money?

- How can the company keep customers from going away so it can make more money?

- How can the company build more brand loyalty so it can make more money?

- How can the company develop policies and procedures, utilize customer relationship management and voice of the customer data pooling . . . and blah blah blah . . . *so it can make more money?*

THE EXTRA MILE:
IT'S WHAT YOU DO

Recently, I stayed at a luxury hotel in California. At the prices they charged, I expected an extraordinarily high level of service. However, I found a plastic card informing me I'd be paying $29.99 a night for internet service. If I'd been staying at the Hampton Inn down the road for $100 a night, internet access would have been free. In addition, there was a large bottle of Evian with a card hanging from its neck reading, "Enjoy for just $9.95," as if I were supposed to think that was an awesome deal. To make matters worse, on the back of the remote control was a sticker warning me that I'd be charged if I stole the remote. This is *not* exceptional customer service. My message to this hotel is that you may be able to perform "cashectomies" for a while, but it is not likely a sustainable model.

The problem occurs when we look at innovation as a way to create new profit centers rather than as a way to deliver better human experiences. If I ran a luxury hotel, I would charge a thousand dollars a night and give every guest a gift basket that included bottled water, delicious snacks, and other small amenities they would appreciate. My clients would never pay extra for internet service. And that remote control? For that kind of money, and the unlikelihood of a remote control heist, I would forgo the warning label that insults my guests' integrity.

The impetus for designing an exceptional customer experience is not to make more money. Customer experience is a derivative of a holistic system that loves and honors the customer. The money will follow. If your customers love you, they will buy more and stay with you longer, all the while referring their friends and family. To achieve this, you cannot look inward. You must look outward at your customers and know their loves and hates. You must understand their customer type. The best companies in the world do exactly this.

EVALUATING CUSTOMER SERVICE:
THE NET CUSTOMER VALUE STRATA

Everybody talks about exceptional customer service, and many if not most people might think they deliver that type of service, but what does exceptional customer service mean in practice? In today's world of hyper-influential social networks and connection architecture, "exceptional" looks far different than it did in the days of the bullying customer service–industrial complex.

To illustrate this point, I created the Net Customer Value Strata. It's organized in layers, or strata, ranging from the death zone to the superstars. Figure 3-1 illustrates the concept of exceptional service in relation to its evil cousins: criminal, bad, sub-baseline, and baseline service.

Figure 3-1. Net Customer Value Strata.

The Death Zone

Criminal Customer Value: At the bottom of the value strata is what I call criminal customer value—for example, the restaurant where the service is terrible, the food is awful and overpriced, and you end up with food poisoning.

Criminals take something of value, and instead of delivering something of value in return, they deliver pain. It would have been better for that restaurant owner to have broken into my home and stolen $100 from my wallet and saved me the indigestion.

This is the death zone, and in time, organizations here always go out of business. Until they do, though, there are tens if not hundreds of thousands of businesses delivering criminal levels of customer value.

Bad Customer Value: The bad customer value stratum also resides in the death zone. These organizations are one step above criminal, but it won't take much of a push—something along the lines of a new competitor, one influential angry customer, or a new step up in technology—to drive them into the abyss. They're a twin-engine airplane with one engine blown and the other overburdened and in need of repair. It's just a matter of time before that engine fails and the plane crashes.

Maybe these organizations are doing things they think will benefit them, like hiring cheaper labor and cutting back on expenses. What they don't realize is that they are so internally focused that they're sacrificing the customer in the process. It's not a matter of if they will fail. It's a matter of when.

Customers are smart. They understand the connection between how much something costs and the experience they should be getting. The baseline level of expectation is what customers universally expect from a product or service. Service below this level is subpar and death for a business. Service above this level is service that exceeds a customer's expectations. Superstar companies reside far above this baseline level, delivering exceptional and relevant human experiences.

The Danger Zone

Sub-Baseline Customer Value: A majority of businesses occupy this stratum. Companies in this stratum might be making money; they might even be growing. The problem is they have a terminal illness and don't know it. These companies may hear about problems and dissatisfied customers, but although they believe they're fixing the issues, they carry on much as they always have. What they are missing is that these "issues" are much larger than they realize and are eating away at their customer base. Usually, but not always, sub-baseline companies sink into the bad and criminal levels of service.

An average business hears from 4 percent of its dissatisfied customers. This means a whopping 96 percent of dissatisfied customers don't tell companies they're unhappy. Plus, 91 percent of dissatisfied customers don't ever come back.[1]

Baseline Customer Value: Every consumer has a baseline level of expectation for a certain product or service. If I check into a Hampton Inn, I expect to pay a low price for a small, clean, and hopefully quiet room. I'm satisfied. But if I only get a small, clean, and quiet room when I check into the Four Seasons, I'm going to be dissatisfied. I'm expecting awesome.

This baseline expectation exists in every industry and with every customer. The problem is that companies think this is the level of customer service they need to be delivering. After all, if customers get what they expect, they'll be happy, right?

Wrong!

If you deliver only what customers *expect*, you will lose them to the competitor that *wows* them. Therefore, the baseline stratum belongs in the danger zone. It's not a guarantee of death, but it's the next closest thing.

For example, the Kindle delivers exactly what you would expect: it's a great product that gives users the ability to read books and provides other convenient functionalities. However, when the iPad was introduced, it was far above the baseline level of expectation across a broad range of customer types. In fact, it was coined the Kindle Killer, because the phenomenal success of the iPad had such a major impact on both sales and market leadership that most people now see the Kindle as an app, instead of a device.

> n 2011, **seven in ten** Americans said they were willing to spend more with companies they believe provide excellent customer service.[2]

The iPad also has *dynamic*—continually improving—value because it has an active and enthusiastic app-developing community, which means it is going to continue to get better. This is incredibly important because the baseline is always changing. Consumer needs and tastes shift, technology changes, market economies rise and fall, and customers want faster and cheaper options. Companies delivering baseline expectations can easily slip down into the death zone without even realizing it.

Recently, I took a twenty-hour international flight on a major international airline. The entire time, I sat in business class and stared in disbelief at a piece of duct tape holding up my tray table.

It was just a little piece of tape, but over the hours it made me wonder about the underbelly of the airplane. What other parts were duct-taped together? What sort of commitment did the airline have to its business?

As I mused, I noticed that several gadgets were broken and one of my side panels had a long grease smear. Then, ten hours into the flight, we were all asleep when several attendants began laughing hysterically literally a few feet away from us without regard for all the sleeping—and paying—passengers. Now awake, we stared at each other in absolute astonishment.

I'll never fly that airline again if I can avoid it, and I doubt many of the other passengers will be rushing to do so any time soon either; the experience was simply that bad. This is a classic example of a company slipping down the strata of customer value. These companies are no longer providing even baseline value. They're approaching the death zone, and, without serious changes, they might not recover.

The Innovation Zone

This area is where it starts to get interesting and, ultimately, what this book will help you achieve. The innovation zone is where you begin to exceed your customers' expectations. You are no longer providing what they expect; instead, you're beginning to provide exceptional customer service. As you reveal and refine your customer types, and therefore learn how to design these exceptional and relevant human experiences for people, you will shift above baseline expectations. The better you get at this, the further your company will rise.

Fair Customer Value: This level is where you begin to exceed expectations. You know what customers expect and you know what they love and hate. As a result, you are now engineering some exceptional customer experiences. You're not finished, but you've begun your trajectory toward superstar status.

Excellent Customer Value: At this point, you're beginning to hone your competitive edge. You are delivering truly exceptional customer service, and the growth and success of your business is taking on a life of its own. Your customers are turning into your marketing machine through social media and word of mouth, and you are rapidly building a reputation as the go-to place for your product or service.

Exceptional Customer Value: This highest tier in the Net Customer Value Strata is where the superstar innovators reside. They are inventing and delivering exceptional and relevant human experiences across a range of customer types throughout the five touchpoints and across both digital and non-digital channels. They're already doing what I'm teaching you to do in this book, and because of it, their growth is exploding.

THE BUSINESS KILLER: PSEUDO-VALUE CLAIMS

"Customer value" is one of the most misused terms in the business world today. The value you provide your customers must be real and relevant, because pseudo-value will kill your business faster than anything I know in our world of hyper-influential social media.

The Customer Value Claim

Companies create a policy for their benefit—to increase profits—but target their appeals to their customers' personal values. For example, take the water bottle company that tells you it has cut back on the percentage of plastic to save the environment. Did the company really do this to save the environment? Or did it cut back on the percentage of plastic to make a cheaper product that saves money but in the process creates an inferior product?

What about resort hotels that ask you to reuse your towels to save the planet? Good for the planet, or good for the hotels? You be the judge. As I see it, we all know that reusing towels saves money, but when hotels misrepresent their intentions—which are far more obvious to the customer than they may realize—they can leave the guest with a bad opinion of them. Clearly the hotels' motive is to save money, and perhaps incidentally save the planet. Be careful how you represent what you're asking of customers.

Forget hyped-up promises. Make sure your value is real because customers can smell the stench of "phony" a cyber-mile away.

Recently, I was staying at a hotel in Indianapolis. (As you may have guessed, I travel for work a lot.) On my dresser was a bottle of water accompanied by a note stating the hotel had made the water available for my convenience for $15. Don't tell me that's convenient! The hotel was attempting to sell overpriced water to increase its profits. In the same hotel, I went looking for a vending machine to buy a bottle of Gatorade. In the corridor was a sign saying that for my convenience, vending machines were located on every other floor. Going up and down stairs and walking through corridors in my boxers to find some Gatorade wasn't convenient for me or anyone else.

The "It'll-Be-Too-Expensive" Claim

Amazingly, some people think providing exceptional customer experiences is more expensive than providing the poor service they're currently giving. A basic financial analysis reveals the depth of this erroneous concept.

Compare the cost of customer acquisition to the benefits of employee satisfaction and productivity. We know that acquiring new customers is far more expensive than keeping current ones. Well, there is a connection between keeping customers and having satisfied employees. Companies that deliver exquisite customer service also offer a far better quality of work life, and their employees are happy. Think about it. Have you ever had a job where you were asked to deliver substandard products and services or to enforce punitive policies? It felt terrible, didn't it? If you have ever been yelled at or scolded by a customer, you know how miserable that can be. Organizations are beginning to realize that there is a direct corollary among organizational profit, quality of work life, and customer satisfaction. Good people seek out good organizations, and organizations that have a high quality of work life attract better talent—and today there's a premium on good talent.

According to an article in the *Harvard Business Review*, one of the biggest challenges today is attracting millennial talent (those born between 1982 and 1996).[3] These young, talented, and educated people were raised with social media. Being hyper-connected isn't new to them; it's the way things are. In fact, many potential millennial employees research the company using social networks before deciding to apply. They want to know the company's reputation before they spend their time and energy applying for a job. Not only are your customers researching you, but so are potential quality employees.

The moral of the story is to deliver exquisite experiences in order to build an amazing reputation. This means you have to create an ecosystem that attracts the best customers and the best employees. This in turn saves you money because delivering exceptional experiences means your customers will stay with you longer and your employees will have a better work life. You will attract better talent, reduce absenteeism, and increase attendance. The benefits, including higher profits, to your organization far exceed just having happy customers. But you must start by looking out toward your customers, not in toward your company's own desires.

> **I** *t is* **six to seven** *times more expensive to acquire a new customer than it is to keep a current one.*[4]

THE NEW MANDATE: EXCEPTIONAL CUSTOMER EXPERIENCE

So what is exceptional customer experience?

Exceptional customer experience means delivering non-fractional human experiences across both digital and non-digital channels throughout a wide range of customer types that are far above the customer's baseline level of expectation.

This service is both dynamic and layered in that it's constantly changing and improving and appeals to a variety of customer types. Don't expect to create one great experience and be done. As your consumers' needs and tastes change, as technology and the market changes, so your innovations need to keep pace.

Blended Experiences: Digital and Non-Digital

Today, rather than clearly delineated digital and non-digital (or physical) channels, companies are building blended experiences. Blended experiences are an important part of the customer journey.

Most companies have delivery silos. For example, an employee working in inbound telemarketing delivers an experience. The warranty department person delivers another experience, as does customer support. Social media and digital marketing deliver yet more and different experiences. As a result of this silo structure, companies deliver fractional solutions.

You must deliver exceptional and relevant customer experiences across all touchpoints and to all customer types. Otherwise, you deliver fractional experiences. Fractional solutions are deficient when competing in our digitally connected world.

Fractional customer service can take an exceptional experience and turn it on its head so your customer never returns. If I walk into an expensive, high-end restaurant, I expect a certain level of service and food. Perhaps my car is valet parked by a friendly, well-dressed young person; I'm greeted by a professional, cheerful host; my wife and I are immediately seated at a table by the window with a view overlooking a lake; and the menu and wine list are impeccable. But then our server smells like cigarette smoke, and he messes up my wife's order so we're not eating at the same time. That's fractional service, and it can quickly kill your business. Exceptional customer service, in contrast, is a holistic experience across all touchpoints and customer types.

It's a rare and successful company that understands that there has to be a master plan that manages each touchpoint across all departments. Your customers' entire experience must be seen holistically, and they must receive exceptional experiences all along the way. This is what today's great companies do.

A client of mine told me this story about buying a beautiful European luxury car. Most people who buy cars like these have a high level of expectation about quality and service, as did Susan. They're educated, successful, and demanding.

The showroom was clean and spacious, and Susan was immediately offered an espresso. Nice start. In the waiting room were comfortable leather seats, and her salesperson was smart, professional, and well dressed. He exuded caring throughout the sales process.

While they waited for various back-office tasks to be completed, the salesperson talked to Susan's children, eliciting details about their sports and academic interests. Every time Susan asked him a question about the car, he professionally and quickly answered it, and then got back to the business of asking about her family. It almost seemed as if he didn't care if he sold her a car; he just wanted to enjoy the human connection.

O*n average, loyal customers are worth* **up to ten times** *as much as their first purchase.*[5]

It was an amazing human experience: Susan, who happens to be the amiable type who wants that level of personal service, bought the car and felt she had made a friend. She purchased her car believing she would receive this same level of personal service throughout the company.

Boy, was she wrong.

A couple of months later, Susan took the car in for its first service. She walked up to the man at the service podium, who was busy writing notes from the customer before her. Several awkward moments followed, then he looked up and brusquely said, "What?" Not even a "hello." Unsure how to respond, she explained that she was there to get her car serviced. He walked away and didn't return for a full fifteen minutes.

Susan told me she will never buy another car from that dealership as long as she lives. She even wrote the experience up on Yelp. Not surprisingly, she wasn't the only one to write about such an experience.

This is a fractional customer experience, and something like this can kill your business. The cost of advertising and promotion to make up for non-repeat business is huge.

T he probability of selling to a new prospect is 5 to 20 percent, while the probability of selling to an existing customer is 60 to 70 percent.[6]

CUSTOMER SERVICE TRAINING AS CURE-ALL: THE MYTH

I would be remiss not to address the quite prevalent myth regarding customer experience and customer service training, which is that everything will be just fine if organizations can just get their customer-facing employees to be nicer to the customer. This attitude is so prevalent as to be epidemic. Leaders assume all customer experience problems—and therefore opportunities—reside in training their customer-facing teams. This thinking is extremely flawed.

Part of the problem involves policies that actually punish the customer. I've seen it thousands of times (and explore it extensively in Chapter 9). Far too many organizations have developed organizationally focused, customer-punitive policies without regard to the impact these policies have on the customers. Have you ever tried to return a product to a retailer only to have an employee tell you all the reasons why company policy says you cannot return it? This happens more often than you might think. Would great customer service training fix this problem? How about if the employee had been trained to say "no" using a positive, chirpy tone of voice? Would that make it better? Of course not!

If great employees are forced to deploy bad policies, they will not be immune from an angry customer's wrath. Worse, depending on their personality type, your good employees will either embrace your attitudes toward your customers or they will leave you. Either is bad for your business.

The following story shows the positive results that come from empowering your employees rather than forcing them to uphold punitive policies that end up damaging customer relationships.

Two sisters were going through the belongings of their recently deceased mother. Needless to say, this was an emotional and stressful time. Among their mother's things was a new pair of Zappos boots that had never been taken out of the box. One of the sisters called Zappos about returning them, unaware that Zappos had a 365-day return policy and more time had passed. Complicating matters further, the sisters had already canceled their mother's credit card and weren't sure how a refund, even if given, could be processed.

To their surprise, the Zappos representative stepped up. She explained the company's return policy but offered to make an exception under the circumstances. And that's not the end of the story; it gets better. A couple of days later, their father received a beautiful bouquet of flowers with a note from "Tamika T & the Zappos.com Family." The sisters and their father so appreciated the gesture and exceptional customer service that they have shopped with Zappos over and over again and have tweeted and blogged about their experience.

Zappos could have rejected their refund request. Instead, the company not only made customers for life but recruited advocates who are now helping do its marketing for it.

Many organizations believe that customer experience training can turn bad employees into good ones. Research shows that companies with bad organizational cultures attract bad people who ultimately deliver bad customer experiences. Painfully simple, to be sure, but it's something to be mindful of because most organizations believe they can fix bad employee behavior by training them to be nice.

THE "SOUL OF THE CUSTOMER" PROGRAM

I have learned that the only way to create a profitable and sustainable training program is sequentially, and the Soul of the Customer program does just that.

Your strategy needs to:

Articulate a beautiful and meaningful mission that attracts good people. Of course, you must act upon that mission and prove that everything you say about it is true. Your stakeholders want to look up to you, and they want to know that you are doing the right thing for customers. Hiring good people means creating an enterprise infrastructure of goodness. Sounds ridiculous, I know. But the best companies in the world have created a culture around treating customers exceptionally well. Because they do this, they attract quality people, and quality people are interested in learning new and exciting ways to deliver better quality and customer experiences.

A bad culture attracts bad people, and as a result, you will deliver bad experiences. Then, in the end, you will be displaced by organizations that deliver good experiences. This is ridiculously simple but incredibly profound.

> **Y**ou should not begin a training initiative until you have identified the gaps in the organization's customer experience infrastructure and culture. Do not attempt to develop a training program until you have created the infrastructure for its success.

I worked with a national fast-food restaurant chain that had historically focused on its restaurants' systems and processes. Very little attention had been paid to the way the front counter staff interacted with customers. I noticed that customers were not being treated in a friendly and engaging way; for example, the counter attendants never smiled at them. I initiated a training program that included teaching the front counter people the importance of smiling and making eye contact. We taught them to acknowledge every person who walked in, thereby changing that important initial moment of contact.

Customize your customer experience training to meet your brand's unique needs. Yes, you are special, and your organization is exceptional. This is why just-add-water strategies never work and why the generic training programs used by hundreds of different companies will never hit the mark for your business. When I am asked for a copy of our training program, I say we don't have one. Instead, we have thousands of *customized* training programs—designed specifically to meet the individual and particular needs of each client, and which now belong to that customer. If someone tries to sell you an off-the-shelf solution . . . RUN!

Just as we can't use generic terms to define customers, we can't use generic processes to define customer service.

I recently had the great opportunity to work with Polaris Industries. They had secured the rights to the Indian Motorcycle brand, and planned to relaunch it in a very big way. I was brought in to interview dealers and create a customized training program that would communicate the brand promise and uniqueness of the Indian brand. Polaris's commitment to truly understanding the needs and opportunities of both its customers and its dealers makes it one of the best companies in America. Polaris understands that its training program has to speak to the uniqueness of the amazing brand.

Motorcycle dealers have many monsters in their mental attics. They harbor preconceived ideas about manufacturers, projections, and expectations. Polaris management took the time to gain unique insights into what types of dealers sold its motorcycles and to understand its dealers' distinct needs. Then, the company put together a program that was relevant across all dealer types by creating pinpointed brand messaging and training programs that spoke specifically to each of those dealer types. The result could only be described as poetry. Training programs for customer-facing teams require an insane amount of research and customization to deliver value to both the enterprise and your customer, but such programs are more than worth it.

Create collaborative environments with customer-facing stakeholders and other key team members. This collaboration should be ongoing and should leverage enterprise social networks and other digital solutions that use game mechanics and social engagement.

No longer is customer experience development about pushing your ideas down to the minions about how a customer should be treated. It just doesn't work. Think about it. Why should employees treat the customer well? Why should they care if the customer hates you? Why should they go the extra mile? If you have not collaborated with them, they will not be engaged or incentivized to participate in the customer experience game because you never taught them the game in the first place, you never socialized it, and, even worse, you never created a way to win it.

When you engage your employees and allow them to take part in the actual development of customer experience programs, they're far more likely to deliver those programs because they've participated in their creation. Most organizations don't provide meaningful incentives—for example, weekly recognition or financial rewards—to improve the quality of the customer experience. Some organizations have regular customer experience breakouts where the team is asked how they could have done things better, and their peers review what their teammates might have done wrong. Being exposed in front of one's peers is a huge incentive for employees to make sure they have made customers happy.

Today, it's not about customer experience training. It's about *customer experience development*. It's about:

- Building a complete and total ecosystem around the customer-centric enterprise.

- Building great cultures where great people want to work.

- Creating collaborative environments that allow the very stakeholders who deploy policies to your customers to help create them.

- Leveraging game mechanics to increase the returns on your customer experience strategy.

Not long ago, I spoke with a CEO about customer experience. His board of directors had suggested that he stop spending time and energy on his weaknesses, and that since he was not an expert on customer experience, he should bring in the right people, give them the right resources, and let them do what they do best. The takeaway: either bring in outside help or hire experts to become part of your team, so you can make customer experience the priority it needs to be.

THE SECRET TO EXCEPTIONAL CUSTOMER SERVICE

If designing exceptional human experiences is the key, why doesn't everyone do it?

One word: *commitment.*

Many people join gyms. This requires signing up and making a financial commitment. Sometimes people even add a personal trainer to the package, requiring an even larger financial commitment. But this alone doesn't mean they achieve physical fitness.

Statistics show that 80 percent of those who join a gym in January stop going by March. They sign up, but they don't show up. Of the remaining 20 percent, there are two types: watchers and workers. Watchers show up but don't do much. They stand around and, well . . . watch. Only workers, a much smaller percentage, are committed to the actual process of getting fit. Workers can do in five minutes what it takes a watcher to do in an hour.

Fitness, like business, means signing up, showing up, standing up, and—most important—never, ever, ever giving up.

To design exceptional, dynamic, and layered human experiences, you must be truly committed. Don't waste your time otherwise. You might have to endure months of pain as you identify customer types and learn how to deliver exceptional customer experiences. But it's in these tough times that you learn more about yourself and build your greatest strengths.

If your organization makes the commitment to sign up, show up, and stand up, you reap the rewards for many years to come. A daily commitment to a smart plan is how all great organizations are built.

At a workshop, someone asked me, "What's the one thing everyone in this room should leave with?"

My answer: Every one of your customers has a baseline expectation. Customers understand the relationship between price and the experience they should be getting. They are smart. Therefore, the way to deliver exceptional customer service is to go far beyond the baseline level of expectation and deliver surprisingly beautiful experiences across a wide range of customer types throughout the five touchpoints both digitally and non-digitally.

That's the secret.

TAKEAWAYS

Shockingly, many experts argue that companies should deliver the *lowest* level of customer experience necessary in order to profitably sell products and services. In fact, there is a whole new range of experts propagating this idea. The thought makes my head explode!

Most organizations that have failed were doing the bare minimum. Were this to become a widely used practice, it would be absolutely toxic. It is a myth that you need to increase costs in order to deliver better human experiences. Exceptional customer service isn't about spending more money. It's about using your creativity and intelligence to invent better experiences.

Don't get me wrong. Sometimes you have to spend more money and work much harder in order to be truly exceptional. The good news is that customer experience superstars that have made this investment have received multiple returns on that investment.

I consult for one of the largest restaurant chains in the world. Its problem is that it cannot make its product any cheaper or any better. The product is as good as it can get. Unfortunately, so are the products of all my client's competition. This leads us to the issue of, when consumers can buy anything at almost any price and still expect almost perfection, how do you differentiate your brand in a way that's meaningful to your customer types? The answer is simple: the secret weapon is your ability to deliver beautiful human experiences, highly targeted to a wide range of customer types. Deliver this range of amazing experiences across each and every touchpoint in both digital and non-digital channels. Creating perfect human experiences is worth the effort because, by doing so, you can expect an exquisite return.

CHAPTER 4

GETTING DOWN TO THE NITTY-GRITTY: *WHY, WHO,* AND *WHAT*

I hope by now I have persuaded you that having a more granular and focused view of the customers you serve is critical to competing in a hyper-competitive market. The more granular your customer view, the more specific your messaging will become and the more targeted your insights will be. Ultimately, having such a view enables you to invent better customer experiences. You send customers on a journey that's been architected for their specific customer type, and as a result you will lead your market in customer loyalty, sales, and profitability.

The greatest companies in the world understand their customers by type (even if they don't call it that), and they serve up exceptional and relevant human experiences for them. Because of this, these companies get significantly better returns on their marketing and customer experience efforts. Their customers can't help but love them because the companies satisfy their core needs and desires. Meanwhile, the rest of the companies face a slow, painful death by competition.

WHAT CUSTOMERS CRAVE
TOP TWENTY FAVORITE COMPANIES

The companies listed below exemplify what it means to under-stand your customer and to invent exceptional experiences across all touchpoints in digital and non-digital channels. Perhaps more important, they have institutionalized the process of gaining real insights about their customers to systematically and predictably deliver exceptional levels of customer value.

❏ Apple

❏ Closet Factory

❏ Costco

❏ Dutch Bros.

❏ Google

❏ In-N-Out Burger

❏ MAC Cosmetics

❏ Nike

❏ Nordstrom

❏ Polaris Industries

❏ Safelite

❏ Salesforce

❏ Southwest Airlines

❏ Sur La Table

❏ Tesla Motors

❏ Trader Joe's

❏ Whole Foods Market

❏ YETI

❏ Zappos

❏ Zoya

These companies understand that, to be competitive in to-day's world, you need to know that it's not customer service—it's customer experience. It's not having inward-driven organizational goals—it's creating outward-driven holistic, relevant experiences for your customers. In return, these satisfied customers will nurture you with sales, repeat business, referrals, and incredibly powerful positive ratings on social media as well as through digital sharing, which creates a digital trail of excellence that drives more sales than any marketing campaign you could ever dream up.

In this chapter. we begin framing up strategies and tactics to help you identify the customer types within your specific business. You will then be able to use these concepts to understand *who* your customer types are, *what* they love and hate, and *why* you should care.

I am often surprised at how poorly developed most organizations' enterprise strategies are. These initiatives ensure that organizations meet their stated goals—for example, achieving better returns on assets, increasing customer satisfaction, and implementing technological innovations. But without an enterprise strategy carefully tied to your customer experience strategy, you will likely fail in today's hyper-competitive economy.

FRAME UP *WHY* YOU CARE

The reason why you care lies in the answer to this basic question: Why are you in business? That, in turn, leads to the answers to these questions: Why should you care about understanding *who* your customers are? And why should you spend all your time and effort in this endeavor when you could be doing (*fill in the blank*) instead?

In working with leadership teams, I use a traditional linear process to help them get down to the tactics of how to create exceptional customer experience strategies. The genesis of this process is to create a one-sentence mission statement. All of your strategic initiatives and certainly your customer experience strategy will derive from this key concept. Because your mission statement essentially asks why you are in business, it defines your reason to exist. To be effective, the statement should be short, powerful, and to the point.

In researching the topic of mission statements, I unearthed an interesting phenomenon. Generally, organizations with mission statements that speak to the organization's needs rather than the needs of its customers and the markets it serves fail at delivering exceptional customer experiences. Not surprisingly, customer service failure results in higher levels of business failure.

For this reason, when you design your customer experience strategy, it's important that you first develop a well-defined mission statement that you can communicate both to your stakeholders and your customers. This is not a marketing issue; rather, it is about defining the foundation for why you are in business. What you do to create amazing customer experiences springs from your mission statement and therefore should encapsulate your organization's overarching values and reason for being.

Here is an example of a bad mission statement: "XYZ Corporation's mission is to drive the most profitable internet company in our market. In addition, our mission is to build an enterprise that delivers the highest returns on investment for our stockholders."

Here are some examples of several great companies' mission statements:

- **Apple** is committed to bringing the best personal computing experience to students, educators, creative professionals, and consumers around the world through its innovative hardware, software, and internet offerings.

- **Facebook**'s mission is to give people the power to share and make the world more open and connected.

- **Google**'s mission is to organize the world's information and make it universally accessible and useful.

- **YouTube**'s mission is to provide fast and easy video access and the ability to share videos frequently.

- **Amazon**'s vision is to be Earth's most customer-centric company; to build a place where people can come to find and discover anything they might want to buy online.

"A customer is the most important visitor on our premises.
He is not dependent on us, we are dependent on him.
He is not an interruption in our work, he is the purpose of it.
He is not an outsider in our business, he is part of it.
We are not doing him a favor by serving him.
He is doing us a favor by giving us an opportunity to do so."
—MAHATMA GANDHI, 1890.

FRAME UP *WHO* YOUR CUSTOMERS ARE AND *WHAT* THEY LOVE AND HATE

You will never have a perfectly architected customer type. People run so deep and are so nuanced that you can't capture it all. Although we aim for precision in identifying customer types and their loves and hates, we can do it only in a less than precise, observational way. It's a sloppy process. Fortunately, though, being perfect doesn't matter. The key isn't to frame up your customer types in terms of perfection but rather in terms of productivity.

When we drill down, we generally find a great deal of overlap from one customer type to another, so even though you might not get it exactly right, you can still benefit because the same things often work for different customer types. In the process of creating specific value for one customer type, you also provide value for another type. Most organizations never drill down to understand their customers this deeply. Therefore, they won't know their customers as well as you will know yours, which will cost them a lot of money and be to your benefit. So, while you might not create the perfect customer type, you will create productive and profitable customer types.

The Anatomy of Customer Types

To simplify the concept of customer typing, I've created an anatomical view of a customer (see Figure 4-1) to illustrate their experiential components. The term "node" describes the customer as they experience a product or service from a sensory perspective. Humans are multisensory, and we gather millions of bits of data every second, including smell, sound, and sight. Through the collection and assessment of these inputs, we determine our overall experience. We then determine the customer type, what they hate and love, and how to best serve them.

I call the three building blocks or key areas of the anatomical view **E**xpectation, **S**ensory Experience, and **P**rice/Value (ESP). Together, they tell you what your customers hate and love. Here's how it works:

1. Customers come to your product or service with an expectation of the experience they will have. You lose if you simply meet that expectation. You must exceed it at each and every touchpoint.

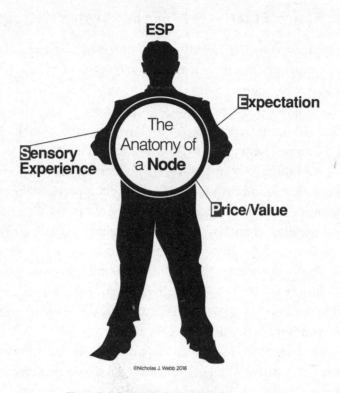

Figure 4-1. Anatomical view of a customer.

2. We all receive information through our senses, such as sight and smell. At each touchpoint, make sure customers are delighted by each sensory experience they have.

3. Finally, what customers expect from a product or service relates to what they pay for it. If your price exceeds the value your customers expect, they will be dissatisfied and leave you. If, on the other hand, you increase the value customers receive by exceeding their expectations and your price is below what they expect, they will become your fans and de facto marketing department.

Design Experiences for Your Customer Types

By understanding your customers' experience in each of these areas more completely, you gain the focus you need to invent experiences for them.

Although I've isolated three specific areas of experience, you still need to make certain you look at the areas combined as a whole and as they pertain to your customer. This is one ingredient that goes into the secret sauce. By understanding the parts, you better understand the whole. If you don't appreciate the whole, you create fractional experiences—a sure recipe for disaster.

In previous chapters, I talked about delivering holistic human experiences throughout the customer journey, that is, throughout the five touchpoints. If you have a beautiful restaurant offering impeccable service but deliver terrible food, you have not delivered a holistic experience; you've delivered a fractional one. And your business will die as a result.

Each of the three anatomical views of the customer—expectation, sensory experience, and price/value—must be considered *at each touchpoint*. This makes your customer experiences amazing, relevant, and holistic. The best innovators in the world deliver the best customer value and lead their markets in profitability and growth by being full-time practitioners of holistic planning.

Here's an example of how this might work: The managers of a hotel realize their new digitally connected customers would like the ability to expedite the check-in process after a long trip. So the managers identify ways to reinvent the check-in process. They might create a Will Call Check-in Station where your keys would be waiting for you when you walked in the door. For the hotel, an ancillary benefit is that such a station would reduce the pressure on the reception desk staff and might even require fewer people there, thus reducing costs. Taking it a step further, the hotel might create a Check-in Welcome Kit that, in addition to the room key, contained free water, instructions for accessing the complimentary Wi-Fi, directions to the gym, and perhaps some healthy snacks.

If the hotel managers did this, they would reinvent the first touchpoint by applying the three anatomical views of the customer: it's an exceptional experience that exceeds their expectation (guests don't have to stand in line and are quickly checked in); their sensory experience is met by the sight of the thoughtful Welcome Kit; and the price/value equation moves in the correct direction as value increases and price stays the same or is even lowered.

One company already doing something like this is In-N-Out Burger, with its exceptional service, clean locations, friendly staff, and appropriately priced burgers. Another is Hollister, with its hip clothes and amazing staff and locations, all without sending prices through the roof. (More about both companies later.)

The Customer Expectation Component

We discussed customer expectations in depth in Chapter 3 with my Net Customer Value Strata (see Figure 3-1 for a quick refresher). But I can't say this often enough: each customer arrives at your product or service with a preconceived expectation of the experience they are about to have. If you deliver at or below that expectation, you fail. It isn't a matter of if, but when. The only question is how long it takes.

What you deliver in terms of products or services doesn't really matter if you don't know what your customers expect. You can have the best product on the planet, but if customers expect something else, it won't much matter because they will be disappointed.

For example, a certain brand of electric skateboards was insanely popular with kids. However, that company's service was extremely poor. Customers found that getting help with a problem or replacing a part was a nightmare. The company's online ratings dropped as a result of negative customer reviews of the customer service. The company's bad reputation then deflected sales to its competitors, which delivered both great technology and great service.

You can't make up for bad customer experiences solely with great technology. Great technology is expected nowadays. Creating exceptional customer experiences is where the battles are fought and won.

Therefore, understanding your customers' expectations across all types, throughout their journey, and across their sensory experience and price/value expectations (see below) is critical to your success.

Exceed the Expected

Your job is to devise products and services that exceed what your customers anticipate. By understanding your customers and what they expect more deeply, you are positioned to deliver products and services well beyond what they imagined. Therefore, being very careful about understanding what your customers *really* expect is another secret ingredient to your success.

From the perspective of sensory experience, if your customers expect your restaurant to smell good, then ask yourself: "What smells good?" Should it smell like bleach to signify cleanliness, or like garlic to signify savory, delicious food? Some customer types may have a negative attitude about bleach; they may think it's covering something up. For some, the smell of garlic is delicious; for others, it's repulsive. A direct function of knowing your customer types is knowing what "good" is.

The same holds true for price/value expectations. Does a higher price relative to competitors' prices mean "better quality" for your customer type? Or does it mean "overpriced rip-off"? While a $100 room at a Hampton Inn may be expensive compared to a Holiday Inn Express, it's incredibly cheap compared to a Four Seasons. What does the customer expect in return? What does the customer expect in terms of their experience at a Hampton Inn versus the Four Seasons?

Understand what your customer expects at each touchpoint. Exceed that expectation in surprising and relevant ways.

The Customer Sensory Experience Component

Human beings are multisensory and glean information from a range of sensors that transmit that information through the central nervous system to the brain, where the data is aggregated. We constantly gather information that we aggregate at lightning speed to form opinions of the overall experience.

Once the sensory data has been aggregated and interpreted, we can then respond. Is this idealistic? No. Is it pragmatic? Yes, and that's what's needed if you are to be successful.

Consumers experience our products, services, and brands through these sensory inputs:

- Sight

- Sound

- Smell

- Touch

- Taste

The best companies in the world make sure their customers have amazing experiences across each of the sensory inputs at each touchpoint.

Multisensory Design

Targeting primarily teenagers and young adults with their Southern California sun and surf theme, the executives at the retailer Hollister understand they're selling a story. The story is that it's attractive to be a young and hip sun-soaked surfer. A subsidiary of Abercrombie & Fitch Co., Hollister tells this story across different sensory inputs and touchpoints, both digitally and non-digitally.

For example, Hollister brilliantly understands that aroma matters. When you approach a Hollister store, you experience its great smell from several shops away. The company has invested in perfume pumps that push the aroma throughout the store, so the pre-touchpoint is already beautifully covered, and customers enter the store with a positive perception.

Next, Hollister hires attractive salespeople whom many teenagers and young adults aspire to look like. Not only do they look great, but they often wear Hollister clothing. The business wants to sell this image to customers.

The visual sensory input doesn't stop there. In an effort to create exceptional and relevant human experiences, the stores are designed to look like they're sitting on the Huntington Beach pier. In fact, a live video feed from the Huntington pier is projected onto both sides of the stores. Hollister has leveraged digital technology to enhance the in-person experience. And, of course, the latest pop music is pumping through an excellent sound system.

With the lighting, scent, music, staff, and live video feed, Hollister has designed a retail experience that makes its customers believe that if they buy Hollister clothes, they're going to be one of the cool surfer kids too.

The retail environment is brilliant. I love this brand because the company put a lot of thought into inventing a bold ambience that provides great human experiences while concurrently driving big sales.

Architecting the Experience to Customers' Sensors

When architecting the physical store experience for your customer, the aesthetics must fit what your customers enjoy. By *aesthetics*, I mean their sensory experiences—the colors, shapes, sounds, and even smells that envelop them as they enter.

For example, music has a powerful ability to influence the mood of both your customers and your floor staff. Once, I went to a jewelry store on Fifth Avenue in New York. The store aesthetic was one of restrained elegance. I noticed the music. It was vaguely classical, very muted and serene. I asked one of the salespeople about it. She smiled and said: "The music is designed exclusively for our store. It's a constantly evolving tapestry that evokes our luxury brand. You won't hear it anywhere else."

I replied that it worked very well.

On the other hand, I was recently at a microbrewery in the San Francisco Bay Area. It played rap music so loudly you could hardly hear the person sitting across from you. The brewery was hip and fun, and music was part of the tapestry of the human experience it delivered. As a result, people lined up outside and around the corner to get into the brewery to listen to the music and drink reasonably good beer.

The takeaway: when you carefully architect experiences for your customer type's sensors, you win every time. The folks at the microbrewery weren't just playing rap music. They were playing it loudly! The type of music and its volume were all part of the brewery's insight into how to deliver relevant experiences to a San Francisco microbrew customer.

The Customer Price/Value Component

What we expect to receive from a product or service is directly correlated to what we pay for it. This experience driver comes into play in every business and with virtually every customer. To ignore it is to perish. If the price is less than the value customers expect, you will increase sales as well as the number of happy customers. If the opposite is true—if the price *exceeds* the value customers expect to receive—they will leave you in droves. I call this the Price/Value Slip, which is illustrated in Figure 4-2. Avoid it at all costs.

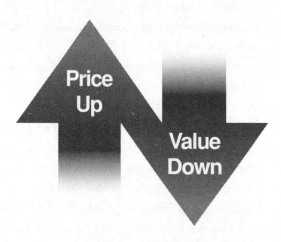

Figure 4-2. Price/Value Slip.

In Chapter 3, I described my customer service experience with a major international airline that was so bad I don't think it could pay me to fly with it again. This company does not understand the Price/Value Slip, and as a consequence, its sales are suffering and it is losing its once-loyal customers. Most organizations go from the start-up to the operational phase; later, they become organizational and bureaucratic and focus on ways to make more money. The Price/Value Slip occurs at this last stage, when the decision makers think it's smart to provide a little less in value and charge a little more for it.

The Price/Value Equation

A great example of the Price/Value Equation can be found in one of my favorite hotel chains—Hampton Inn, as you may already have guessed. I travel to nearly forty events a year worldwide, giving talks on innovation, business leadership, and customer experience. As a result, I'm a pretty savvy traveler. I've experienced the very best hotels and the very worst.

Hampton keeps its prices surprisingly low, yet with all the free amenities it offers, for which I usually have to pay extra elsewhere, the hotels feel upscale. Hampton generally delivers a great experience at a competitive price. The bottom line is that the organization delivers more than what I expect, which is why it is one of my favorite hotels.

All customers have an expectation of what they should receive for the money they spend. In terms of hotels, the Motel 6 chain is at the very low end of the scale. Its

> *customers expect a very inexpensive room that's clean. If I paid $500 and was delivered a Motel 6 experience, I would be offended. Conversely, if I were a cross-country truck driver, the cost of a hotel room comes out of my profits. Since what I want is some much-needed rest in a clean room for $49, I would think Motel 6 was an excellent value.*

The price/value equation demonstrates price sensitivity for products and services based on what the consumer is expecting. One of the biggest mistakes most organizations make is that they tend to increase their prices at the same time as they (intentionally or unintentionally) reduce the value they deliver.

> **T**he difference between customers' expectations of their experience and what they receive equals their perception of that brand. If they receive more than what they expect, they walk away with a positive perception. If they receive less than what they expect, you can do the math. It's not pretty.

FRAME UP THE BEST HUMAN EXPERIENCES ACROSS TOUCHPOINTS

I believe that In-N-Out Burger is the best fast-food restaurant chain in the world. Why? The company not only delivers an exquisite product—a delicious burger—it delivers exceptional human experiences across each touchpoint throughout a wide range of customer types in both digital and non-digital channels.

Let's examine the experience touchpoint by touchpoint.

The Pre-Touch Moment

Before you ever even engage with this amazing restaurant, you smell it blocks away. Enormous exhaust fans push the delicious burger smells out into the streets. It's no accident; rather, it's the beginning of the customers' journey. Your sense of smell, one of the most powerful sensations, is immediately engaged in a positive and stimulating way.

As this incredible smell excites your taste buds, you approach the restaurant and note that the property is perfectly maintained. When you look into the windows, you see an immaculately clean restaurant with professional-looking and spotlessly dressed employees. This preengagement visual story communicates to customers that In-N-Out Burger is serious about quality and sanitation. So, even before the customer has entered the restaurant and ordered, In-N-Out—through sight and smell, two extremely important drivers to consumers of fast food—is already delivering an exceptional experience. By the time the customer orders their food, they have a positive impression tucked away in their mind.

The experience is holistic at this point. All the parts go together.

The First-Touch Moment

In-N-Out began as a drive-through chain, and this is still the most common first-touch point. As you enter the drive-through, you see a simple yet captivating menu. What you don't see is In-N-Out trying to be everything to everybody. It is a specialist, with a mission statement centered on delivering the best burgers and fries in the world. It is extremely good at delivering on that promise.

At the drive-through, you're greeted by an intelligent order taker who judiciously repeats your order to make sure they have it right. Drive-through patrons may not notice, but a tremendous amount of time, effort, and resources have gone into the acoustics of In-N-Out's drive-through speaker system. In fact, when the business was launched in the 1950s, In-N-Out actually used megaphones to make sure the order taker could clearly hear the customer and that person could clearly communicate back to them. The quality two-way communication at the drive-through increases accuracy (a big deal in fast food) and also improves the consumer experience.

Beautiful building, clear and simple menu, and a good, crisp, audible dialogue with an intelligent and engaged employee: a great first-touch.

The Core-Touch Moment

In-N-Out Burger is such a great restaurant that it's almost become a cult in California. People drive extra miles to get to one, bypassing dozens of other fast-food joints along the way.

In fact, if you're in the inner circle of In-N-Out Burger patrons, you're probably familiar with the "secret menu." It is "secret" because it's not displayed on the drive-through menu, only on the website. From this secret menu you discover off-menu items like the Flying Dutchman Animal Style burger and the Neapolitan milkshake, which you can then go and order at the restaurant.

The secret menu (and super-secret menu—just Google it) gives customers a sense of belonging to a special club. In this way,

In-N-Out can provide a broader range of options and still keep its core menu crisp and clean.

The Last-Touch Moment

The last-touch for In-N-Out Burger comes when you pick up your order at the window. A smart, well-trained employee greets you and double-checks your order to make sure it's right. Your amazing-smelling food is delivered in special boxes that make it easy to eat while driving. If you prefer, the food can be put in a bag to keep it fresher longer while you take it back to your home or office.

Employees consistently engage you in a way that suggests they truly care and are glad to serve you. The last-touch is a sincere smile from a great team member. Well done, In-N-Out Burger. No wonder it's the best fast-food restaurant chain in the world.

The In-Touch Moment

In-N-Out has a creative and unique in-touch experience. Once customers know about the secret menu and the super-secret menu, they frequently refer to them to find interesting menu items only they know about. In a twist on the traditional in-touch experience, customers are inspired to stay in touch with one another. This menu discussion seems to occur organically—I'm not sure how much involvement In-N-Out has—and it is a magical in-touch experience.

CAUTION:
BEWARE A FRACTIONAL CUSTOMER EXPERIENCE

What would happen if In-N-Out Burger provided most of all this, but one of the sensory inputs delivered a bad customer experience?

Let's say, for example, that everything was as I described it above, but this time the smell from the restaurant seemed suspiciously bad. Something just wasn't right. Would you go back? Would you tell your friends that you had a great experience or that they should watch out since something wasn't right?

All it takes is one broken link in the chain to turn a great experience into a terrible one. This is the difference between hugely successful companies and those in the slow slide to oblivion.

The takeaway is simple: the best brands in the world deliver exceptional human experiences that include all sensory inputs, for all customer types, throughout digital and non-digital channels.

Without this customer experience savvy, In-N-Out Burger would be just another fast-food joint. Hollister, which I talked about earlier, would be just another retail store selling trendy clothes to young adults. It's the ability to deliver at each touchpoint, across all sensors, for all your customer types that creates exceptional human experiences.

PUTTING IT TOGETHER:
WHAT YOU NEED TO KNOW ABOUT YOUR
MULTIDIMENSIONAL CUSTOMER

There are four things you need to know about your customers:

1. What they like and hate across each and every sensor.

2. How to target them across their price/value sensitivity.

3. What their expectations are across each and every touchpoint.

4. How to reach them across both digital and non-digital channels.

Knowing your customer types is extremely important, especially because your competitor is probably too lazy to do the hard work required to gain these insights.

I've spent a quarter-century in the new product development space and as a business developer and inventor with more than forty U.S. patents. What I've discovered is that the many (and there have been many) mistakes I've made were caused by my attempts to take a product to market before doing the heavy lifting required to understand my customer types. If only I knew then what I know now. If only!

"Spend a lot of time talking to your customers face to face. You'd be amazed how many companies don't listen to their customers."
—ROSS PEROT

Is it really worth spending the time and effort to identify your customer types and invent exceptional and relevant human experiences across their customer journey? Yes, yes, and yes!

Just sift through stories of the countless business start-up failures, and you will see in their wreckage people who simply didn't know their customers. Statistics show that 85 percent of consumer products fail in the market because the businesses didn't know their customers. Less than 2 percent of the three thousand patents issued each week by the U.S. Patent and Trademark Office ever make it to market.

I believe the overwhelming reason for failure in product and service businesses is a squishy understanding of their customers and the experiences delivered to those customers.

The Return on Your Investment

I could literally write a five-hundred-page book inventorying the incredibly bad news of how organizations fail because they do not know their customers and their customers' expectations. But I think it's more interesting to point out the benefits that better insights into your customers will provide you and your enterprise.

With better insights, you will:

- Significantly reduce product and service launch failures.

- Significantly increase customer retention and satisfaction.

- Improve the quality of your employees' work life.

- Reduce the cost of customer acquisition.

- Build and monetize brand value.

- Fuel all new product activities with better insights.

- Reduce time to market.

- Increase new product development throughput.

- Reduce advertising and promotion costs.

- Attract and retain the best talent, including the all-important millennial talent.

- Attract better vendors and better vendor relationships.

- Improve distribution and channel options.

- Increase sales.

- Reduce marketing and operation costs.

- Significantly improve returns on all strategic initiatives.

TAKEAWAYS

We become great when we learn to collaborate with our customers. Unfortunately, too many companies have been built on a hierarchical, authoritarian structure. In the early days, we pushed out one-way dialogue to customers in the form of persuasive advertising. Those days are gone for good. Our customers want to be part of the conversation, and they want to work in partnership and engage with brands in an authentic way.

In-N-Out Burger did not create its secret and the super-secret menus for its customers to dictate to them, but because the restaurant knows its customers love to be part of its digital inner circle and share new and exciting secret menu items. Nobody was trying to sell anything to anybody. The menus occurred because a genuine dialogue in the digital sandbox was created organically within the restaurant's enthusiastic fan base.

One of the people I admire most is Ken Grossman, the founder and CEO of Sierra Nevada Brewing Company. Ken loves beer, and after the forty-plus years he's been in business, he still really, really loves his customers. As a result, he collaborates with them. Every year there is a contest among his enthusiastic fans to participate in his annual Sierra Nevada Beer Camp. If you Google "Sierra Nevada Beer Camp," you find videos of people getting Sierra Nevada tattoos, singing Sierra Nevada songs, and doing anything and everything they can to collaborate and connect with the brand.

When was the last time one of your customers went out and got a tattoo with your logo on it? Ken has dozens of customers walking around with Sierra Nevada tattoos. When was the last time one of your customers wrote you a song and shared it online for millions to see?

Being exceptional requires maintaining authentic contact with your customers. Unfortunately, most organizations leverage email addresses and try to trick customers into giving them contact information so they can later use it to spam the latest offer. But staying in touch with your customers is about providing a continual stream of free value. It is not about hijacking their contact information and selling them stuff. Instead, listen to your customers. Get to know their loves and hates and design authentic and continual forms of customer engagement.

CHAPTER 5

INNOVATING EXCELLENCE

So what does innovation have to do with delivering world-class customer experiences? The old days of inventing bright, shiny objects to bring in more sales have given way to disruptive innovators using a powerful range of tools to out-invent their competition. It's through this innovation that we build out amazing customer experiences. We gain actionable insights and then turn them into beautiful experiences across a wide range of customer touchpoints.

If innovation is the secret weapon—and it is—then *how* do we innovate?

I've been directly involved in innovation for a quarter of a century. Over the years, my consulting business has practically turned into an "innovation hazmat team" because we spend most of our time mopping up after failed innovation initiatives.

The good news is that I've learned an enormous amount about why innovation fails in most organizations. Put bluntly, I've seen so many innovation disasters that I can tell long beforehand what will work and what won't. From this experience and knowledge, I have developed a very simple system that ensures innovation success every time.

It's easy to dismiss the need to develop an innovation infrastructure in your enterprise because, after all, you've made it this far without one. If you believe that the marketplace is not disruptive and that customers are not demanding more, then perhaps you can dismiss the need to innovate.

But for 99.9 percent of businesses, this isn't the case. In fact, there is a direct corollary between incremental innovation and mediocre customer experience.

THREE SIMPLE STEPS TO DRIVING INNOVATION

I've boiled down what I've learned into a three-step system for driving innovation excellence. While it took me years to understand and develop these steps, like the best inventions, they've turned out to be surprisingly easy to implement.

Step 1:
The Innovation Readiness Assessment

If you went to your doctor and she prescribed a heart medication without doing any tests or examining you, you would justifiably be suspicious. How about your mechanic? You bring your car in for service and, without even looking under the hood, he claims you need a new transmission. Unless the doctor or mechanic has some sort of X-ray vision, you would turn around and walk out.

The same is true of organizations. You cannot set up an innovation program without first doing a thorough assessment and diagnosis of the problems you are trying to solve and what is currently being done about them. To determine if your organization is ready for an innovation program and what it should look like, you need to start with a good assessment.

Surprisingly, most organizations begin work on innovation without doing a complete and thorough self-examination. Remember, innovation is a delicate ecosystem consisting of hundreds of moving parts, including customer types, expectations, sensory input, price/value sensitivity, collaborative environments, and so on. To succeed, you must have the systems, methods, tools, and processes necessary to make innovation *real* in your enterprise.

Getting Ready for Your Readiness Assessment

Sometimes you can accomplish a task on your own, and other times you've got to have expert help. For example, for years I tried to get in shape and lose weight, but with no sustained success. I followed the diets and the fitness programs, and nothing truly stuck. I always reverted to where I'd started from, or worse. It wasn't until I hired an expert—a fitness trainer who had the outside perspective, training, and experience necessary to help people like me—that I was able to make fitness and health real and long lasting.

Likewise, I have found it best in business to have an outside expert conduct an innovation readiness assessment (sometimes called an innovation gap analysis). For most organizations, it is critical that the assessment be done by a company that specializes in innovation best practices. These companies have trained experts with an outside perspective. Just like my fitness program, for best results, it needs to be done from the outside looking in.

A client told me that before his organization reached out to me, it had conducted its own self-assessment. Here's how he

characterized it: "Conducting your own innovation readiness assessment is kind of like doing your own tonsillectomy. It's going
to hurt and you're not likely going to have a good outcome."

Should you decide to do your own assessment, first get training on innovation best practices to get a good perspective on
what's really required. Meaningful customer training is essential
because none of us is born an expert in customer experience; we
need to develop the skills. Most organizations hire really great
people to do customer service but then shove them out without
any training. All training should be customized to the unique
needs of your organization and should be specific to the job title;
for example, sales staff should get one type of training, while executives get another.

On the other hand, so-called innovation gurus are popping up
everywhere, so make sure you choose wisely. The last thing most
organizations need is to bring in a new level of bureaucracy, because bureaucracy is the enemy of innovation. Hire a company
that has experience mopping up failed initiatives, and avoid any
company that has a just-add-water solution. No one-size-fits-all
template will work. In our innovation management consulting
practice, we have a simple process: understand the client, build
out an innovation roadmap, and then assist in its execution. This
process offers the lowest risk with the highest return.

When I was a young man, I traveled to Zurich. Naturally, I had
to buy a Swiss watch while I was there, which gave me the opportunity to talk to a Swiss watchmaker, a man with a tremendous
body of knowledge and expertise related to the inner workings of
clocks and watches. In the center of his store was a massive clock.
The front was completely clear so you could see the intricate
workings of this mechanical masterpiece.

The watchmaker talked about watches (and clocks) as delicate ecosystems. He told me that with any slight variation in

mechanical tolerances, two things could happen, both bad: (1) The watch would come to a complete stop. Actually, he proclaimed, "Stopping is good," explaining that when a watch stops, it's telling you that it's broken, and you are prompted to get it fixed. (2) The watch would continue to run, but unbeknownst to the owner, it would no longer be accurate. The owner would assume all was well, and therefore the watch wouldn't get repaired until the owner missed an important appointment!

And that's where the danger lies. Innovation is like a watch or clock. It has hundreds of moving parts. If these moving parts are not all working in synchronicity, your innovation ecosystem collapses.

Many organizations have ticking watches and therefore assume they are being innovative. For example, a company's new website might be attracting online customers, so the company incorrectly believes its entire innovation system is optimized and the information gleaned from the market is correct. The company assumes the methods of developing innovation are ticking along nicely, only to find itself blindsided by an existing or emerging competitor.

I would never dream of trying to tinker with my watch. It's too complex. I know it requires an outside expert who understands the hundreds of moving parts and how to optimize them. Innovation programs also have moving parts that come together in a formal innovation governing structure. Like my watch, innovation programs are complex. Most organizations execute an innovation without going to an expert. Such organizations often omit the diagnostic and developmental stages and are not optimized through innovation best practices. Yet this is exactly what's needed for best results. For this reason, proper innovation is typically designed and implemented using outside experts.

Step 2:
The Innovation Roadmap

Based on your innovation readiness assessment, you've determined that you have the correct resources, systems, and talent in place to get started. You also have determined where your innovation gaps are.

The next step is creating your innovation roadmap. Surprisingly, the overwhelming majority of organizations looking to drive enterprise collaboration and innovation never actually create an innovation plan. "Failing to plan is planning to fail," as the saying goes, and this is certainly true when it comes to innovation.

My guess is that if you were planning to hire a vice president of finance, you would first carefully assess her qualifications, training, and experience relative to financial control and leadership. Then you would have detailed discussions about where you wanted the company to head and how you envisioned getting there.

Yet most stakeholders charged with the responsibility to execute on innovation have little or no training specific to innovation best practices. Building a roadmap is a key element of those best practices. This is why it's so valuable to hire or have trained stakeholders who understand the working parts of innovation best practices.

M y guess is you would not allow someone who just "felt" he was a natural born surgeon perform even minor surgery on you. You would probably run—fast and far—in the opposite direction. Surgeons must complete years of training to make certain they know what they are *doing. Innovation is no different. It requires specific learned skills. Organizations that do not provide innovation training and coaching fail.*

Design an Innovation Roadmap

Once you have completed a comprehensive innovation readiness assessment, do yourself a favor and take the time to build out a roadmap that is customized to the uniqueness of your organization. Make sure not to skimp on how you build it. *Good innovation initiatives provide significant and predictable returns on investment.*

Studies show that the main reason innovation initiatives fail is that they were not surgically connected to the enterprise strategy. In designing your innovation roadmap, it is essential to make certain you're using innovation as a way to serve your stated enterprise goals.

Step 3:
Innovation Execution and Measurements

In medicine, the correct medical pathway is for the doctor to perform a thorough assessment and diagnosis, develop a focused and quality treatment plan, and ultimately deploy and measure the treatment and results.

This linear, step-by-step approach makes great sense. It is also the perfect process for winning in innovation. Once you've completed your innovation readiness assessment and developed your comprehensive innovation roadmap, the final phase is execution and measurement. For this, you must determine how you're going to measure success, fill all of your resource gaps, and launch with sustainable determination.

Different sources quote different ways of measuring innovation success. Some have three essential ways, while others have ten. For the sake of simplicity, I suggest measuring innovation success by determining how much it helped you improve a specific strategic initiative. How much better are you as a result of using that innovation best practice? For example, if your goal was to reduce cost, by how much was it reduced? For our purpose, we're talking about how much an innovation has helped you improve the quality of the experience you've delivered to customers across their journey.

> *Innovation is a lot of fun and is naturally connected to the state of being human. We are creators. That's what we do in the process of deploying innovation, and it's incredibly exciting and rewarding.*

The Six Cs of Innovation Success

During my years as a management consultant, I've been involved in many innovation initiatives. I've discovered there are six elements, which I call the Six Cs, that must be in play for any innovation program to succeed. Below, I walk you through each of the six elements needed to bring a successful innovation program to your organization.

Complete: I believe 90 percent of all innovation programs fail because they are incomplete. As with watches and clocks, the innovation ecosystem is a delicate one. The various species of success must all be alive and well or your ecosystem will collapse.

In other words, you need innovation governance, training, systems, processes, tools, and technologies in place and ready to go. Leave something out and innovation becomes nothing more than a logo and a corporate buzzword. Your innovation readiness assessment, done properly, will make sure you have everything you need to be successful.

Customized: Every industry is different, as is every organization within that industry. Run from the purveyors of the one-size-fits-all solution. Innovation has to be handcrafted to align with your organization's appetite for risk and opportunity and your specific and unique customer types.

It also has to be culturally aligned and realistic in terms of your objectives and how you measure success. By doing a complete innovation readiness assessment, you gain the insights necessary to know how to customize your innovation initiative to fit the unique and special needs of your enterprise and customers.

Culture: This is the life support system of innovation. If your organization is risk-centric and fears collaboration internally and externally, your innovation program is doomed. If you have a fear-based, noncollaborative culture, then chances are you have many other problems related to enterprise success.

Today, organizations need to attract millennial talent. They need to cocreate and collaborate, and ultimately they need to innovate. To do that, you have to be willing to "encourage courage." Get your culture right because it's the new enterprise mandate.

Collaborate: As an inventor, I know that very few innovators have created anything completely on their own. One way or another, people worked together to create that new product or service.

Most people fear collaboration because they're afraid someone else will take credit. In some cases, they're afraid somebody will outright steal their idea. However, I have learned that the best innovators are the ultimate collaborators.

Develop collaborative environments within your organization, create places and times for people to exchange ideas and innovate, and ultimately make collaboration part of your organization's culture.

Connect: Being connected is an often used phrase, but in most organizations, people rarely have important relationships with others. However, innovation and collaboration require being connected. One of the best ways to stay connected is through technology, such as enterprise social networks and similar platforms.

You can also conduct brainstorming sessions, create innovation labs, and have other ongoing innovation activities. Deploy these tools to get creative people together sharing ideas and experiences and to help find more opportunities to invent exquisite customer experiences.

Customer-Centric: Essentially, there is a philosophical difference between organizations that master customer service and experiences and those that fail to do so. Innovation success derives from customer-centric organizations; innovation failure stems from those that are company-centric.

It's paradoxical, but the more you focus on delivering internal enterprise benefits, the less you focus on your real enterprise benefit, which is a loyal customer. The more you focus outward, on your customer, the more inward success you eventually have.

As an inventor, I love watching the TV program Shark Tank. What primarily interests me is how shockingly naïve we are—the "if you invent a new mousetrap the world will beat a path to your door" kind of naïveté. Turns out there have been hundreds of new patents filed on the good old-fashioned mousetrap, and yet only a handful have ever *been commercially successful. Most people are answering questions that nobody's asking.*

Don't be an amateur innovator with your customer experience initiative. Be a disruptive innovator, one who has gained the best insights about what customers really care about and then delivers beautiful experiences across every touchpoint.

INNOVATION:
RISKS AND REWARDS

Every new human experience delivered to customers by a technology or service is an innovation. The way in which we architect these technologies and services is nothing more than an innovation created to deliver differentiated value to a range of customer types throughout a customer journey.

One way to look at the risks associated with innovation is to think of innovation as you would a stock portfolio. Incremental innovations are like low-risk, low-value stocks. In exchange for their low risk, they produce low monetary value. Incremental innovations are low risk and correspondingly deliver low customer and enterprise value.

The best innovators create a portfolio of high-risk, high-reward, disruptive (or breakthrough or landmark) innovations in combination with incremental innovations. As you're looking to invent new experiences for your customer, look across the range of innovation values to deliver innovation that spans the gamut of innovation risk and reward.

Incremental vs. Disruptive Innovation

The problem with most organizations is that their innovations are essentially accidental. Because these organizations have no formal process around innovation, they are not able to create high-value differentiated innovations for their customers. The bigger problem is that most of these organizations create nothing more than incremental improvements to an existing system or process.

Netflix did not invent better videotape or DVDs. The company did not make one small incremental improvement. Instead, it created an entirely new way to deliver affordable, high-quality, high-resolution movies on demand.

Netflix didn't get stuck at the incremental level of innovation value. Instead, it leaped to the top as a disruptive innovator, completely changing the way we experience renting movies. And it reaped a mighty lot of rewards because of it.

In the fast-moving, high-demand, ultracompetitive markets we do business in, we need to create innovations that are both breakthrough and disruptive. In other words, we need to go beyond incremental improvements made to existing experiences to create new experiences that completely displace what went before.

Innovation, like so many other things in business, requires rolling up your sleeves and getting to work. Examining the total process of developing an innovation program is beyond the scope of this book, but I want to make it clear that innovation is required if your organization is going to master customer experience. Some of you may already have successful innovation initiatives underway. For those who don't, I strongly suggest you begin this powerful best practice.

TAKEAWAYS

Remember, whether you're selling a product or a service, you are in the customer experience business. Customer experience is not just a function of training your staff; it's a design function. If you want to design something that's going to succeed, it needs to deliver value to customers across each and every touchpoint.

Innovation is as much a philosophy as it is a business discipline. The philosophy begins with a customer-centered view of the universe. A fractional approach will result in failure, and even worse, you will lose credibility. Don't deploy on innovation until you really mean to carry it through, and when you do, make sure you do it right. When you launch innovation initiatives, build in dashboards and measurements so you can see what's working and what's not. Build a team culture that encourages courage. Put structures in place that help you gain better insights from your customer-facing stakeholders. Beware of "just-add-water" innovation programs, because there is no such thing as a successful cookie-cutter approach toward winning at innovation.

Make your innovation initiative a beautifully handcrafted, custom program that fits the unique and special goals and culture of your business. Don't forget, this is really a lot of fun, so make it buoyant, engaging, and worth your team's effort.

CHAPTER 6

INNOVATION:
A COLLABORATIVE PROCESS

As you've seen, customer typing is an incredibly powerful way to get to know your customers at a deeper level than customer segmentation ever did. As you begin to distinguish among your customer types, your perspective on how you view customer expectations changes. You are able to see the world through your customers' eyes, from their range of experiences, and in coordination with what's important to them—that is, what they love and what they hate. In return, this affects the way you understand and design the experiences you create for them.

In the simplest of terms, you are in the business of customer experience. It doesn't matter if you are selling a product or a service. It doesn't matter if you are a business-to-consumer (B2C) or business-to-business (B2B) enterprise. You are in the business of providing experiences to customers; we all are.

As we've stated, in order to create outstanding experiences, we need to innovate. Each business is unique and each customer type is unique. Therefore, each consumer experience should be tailored to this uniqueness.

Collaboration is a primary driver of innovation and is one of the most important things you can do to gain a competitive edge. I worked with a large computer manufacturer whose service team constantly experienced a product flaw: the USB battery door kept breaking off. The problem was caused by how consumers handled the product, expecting durability, as opposed to how the design engineers handled it, which was with great care. Because there was no collaboration between the design team and the service team, the problem grew worse. Collaboration between the two teams would have quickly led to a solution.

Companies that excel at creating exceptional human experiences collaborate across a range of roles, both internal and external to their organization—for example, vendors, competitors, and employees. These roles can also be broken down into customer types. Understanding each type of collaborative customer will help you create the best innovations for them. As you innovate exceptional experiences for these collaborative customers, your "paying customers" also benefit because you will now be providing them with an improved holistic business experience from top to bottom.

WHAT COLLABORATION CONTRIBUTES TO THE INNOVATION PROCESS

In order to create incredible solutions for your customers, you need to connect and collaborate with others. We can't be all things to all people in the innovation process. We can't know everything, have the most training in every area, and have the most creative ideas alone.

Primary Collaborative Types

Exceptional innovation requires bringing in particular life skill sets and new insights from different collaborators in order to increase the likelihood that our innovations will deliver the highest level of customer value. I have broken down these collaborators into four common customer types. You may have others, but this is an excellent place to start. Figure 6-1 depicts the main collaborative types with whom you can design exceptional and relevant customer experiences.

Figure 6-1. The four primary collaborative customer types.

Each collaborative customer type brings a unique and important contribution to how you create superb experiences across each touchpoint of the customer journey. Each type has a different perspective on the journey and fulfills a different role. By viewing collaborative experiences and expectations from each of these angles, you get a far clearer and more complete picture of the kind of design you need.

Too many organizations become "idea bullies." They assume that they know it all and can do it all. Because they have this limited mindset, they typically end up creating incremental innovations that have little to no customer value.

At the other end of the spectrum, the most successful organizations are collaborators. Years ago, I had the great honor of touring DreamWorks Pictures in California, where I was told a fascinating story about a place they call the Secret Room. (This was many years ago, and I hope my memory is correct.) Apparently, animators wanted a place to collaborate, a place where they could hang out and share ideas undistracted. One day, one of the animators walking to work noticed an outcropping on a section of the building he worked in. On investigation, he found a large unfinished area, where the animators began hanging out at all hours. Creative people aren't creative only between nine and five. Day by day, week by week, the animators brought more things into this space: a fake fireplace and a bar, a menorah and a Christmas tree, and all kinds of furniture.

Eventually, management found out—and *fired* them. They had done all this without permission and had violated all sorts of regulatory codes.

Pretty quickly, though, the managers realized they'd fired some of their best people and hired them all back. They also upgraded the room so it was compliant with the building codes, and to keep the room secret from other employees, added a door that looked like a bookcase. You had to pull on *War and Peace* to gain entry!

My point is that people want to collaborate, especially those doing cool, creative things. Great organizations honor their people by allowing them to do things they do naturally. They seek to cocreate so they can deliver bulletproof innovations and human experiences that lead their market and industry. They are open to skills and experiences from different areas so they can design more holistic experiences for their consumers.

THE CONSUMER COLLABORATIVE TYPE

Up to this point, I've talked about inventing exceptional and relevant experiences *for* your customer. However, it's also important to actively invent *with* your customer. The consumer collaborative type is one of the most important collaborators in your innovation strategic alliance.

There are many ways to cocreate with your customers. We'll discuss the four most important ways here.

The Digital Sandbox:
Listen, Learn, Apply

Southwest Airlines had a popular blog that was entitled *Nuts About Southwest*. The blog allowed Southwest customers, who were referred to as Fans, to express what they loved and hated about their travel experiences with Southwest.

Because the airline is a customer-centric company, its personnel actually listened to the dialogue on this blog (what I call strategic listening) and then applied what they learned from it to their operation.

Most executives believe it is risky to set up digital sandboxes where your customers can openly discuss what they love and hate about your brand. But the opposite is true: it's an excellent way to gain real-time, authentic insights. Your customers can clue you in to areas that need improvement, and more important, they can tell you how you can improve them, which allows you to provide the most exceptional and relevant experiences.

Online Challenges:
Inexpensive and Actionable

Online challenges are another way to collaborate with your customers. Here, you significantly reward customers for presenting ideas on how to improve their experience at various touchpoints. This is a low-cost way to get actionable innovations straight from the horse's mouth.

An added benefit is that your customers will feel involved and that their needs are being heard. This, in turn, creates more ownership and empowerment and leads to increased loyalty—a win for everyone. You don't have to create these online challenges from scratch; there are many "just-add-water" solutions. Examples are Yammer, Spigit, and Bright Ideas.

Online challenges do not involve only external customers. In fact, 80 percent of corporations in the Fortune 2000 use internal social networks. These intranets allow different types of people throughout the organization to hang out together. They're designed to leverage game mechanics and social engagement and can be very much like Facebook. Employees are encouraged to collaborate around organizational needs, problems, and opportunities.

For example, a challenge for an automotive service company might ask for ideas on how to increase the speed of getting customers through the registration and check-in process. A game can be made of it, because people like to win. The challenge provokes discussion and dialogue and can be continually updated. This kind of thing, which is often referred to as internal crowdsourcing, certainly demonstrates the power of collaboration. You might be surprised at how many great ideas your company stakeholders have.

Innovation Safaris:
Live the Experience

As I discussed in Chapter 2, to truly understand your customer types and what they are experiencing, you must go out and live their experiences at each touchpoint. I call these journeys "innovation safaris."

It's essential to get out of your cubicle and spend time every week experiencing each and every touchpoint from your customer's perspective; this is the nut of the innovation safari. Make a commitment to leave each safari with a new customer-centered innovation in mind. If you do this every week for a year, you'll have more than fifty customer-centric innovations to choose from, improve, and implement. It will change your business. It will change your life.

Customer Brainstorming Meetings:
Feedback + Ideas = Innovation

Invite your full range of customer types to formal brainstorming meetings with specific goals to create new innovations across both digital and non-digital channels. Get their feedback and their ideas, and tap into new areas of creativity.

The magic is that you get to hear all this from the people who matter the most: your customers. It's not a focus group where you ask questions about their experiences, take away the information, and collate it with all your other "big data." Instead, it's a structured environment in which you ask them for specific ideas. Tap into their loves and hates, and they will teach you what to innovate.

"Your most unhappy customers are your greatest source of learning."
—BILL GATES

THE STAKEHOLDER COLLABORATIVE TYPE

After the customer, the stakeholder is next in importance. In this context, your stakeholders primarily include your employees.

Generally, enterprise goals are designed to meet well-defined strategic objectives, such as increasing efficiency, reducing costs, finding new innovations, and improving customer relationships. These key employee stakeholders are important because they are **problem-**, **opportunity-**, and **customer-**facing. They're on the front line in dealing with real customers and real issues. They know more about how to deliver on your enterprise strategy than you do.

Collaborating with your employees has tremendous, often untapped, enterprise value that includes but is not limited to the following:

- Significant improvement in the quality of work life.

- Faster time-to-market.

- Better experiences across the customer journey.

- Best touchpoint-specific innovations.

- Lower-cost customer acquisition.

- Improved ability to attract millennial talent.

And the list goes on and on and on.

Stakeholders drive your best innovations. My consulting firm was recently engaged by an organization whose inbound sales had suddenly taken a 15 percent drop. Before hiring us, the company had brought in several consulting firms to look at its pricing strategy, do a competitive analysis, and study market trends to determine what had gone so desperately wrong.

But after spending more than $2 million and four months' work, there was still no answer.

Knowing the history, we went right to the smart and engaged people we needed to speak to: the company's employees. After interviewing only a handful of these important stakeholders, we discovered the problem right under their collective noses.

I asked the first stakeholder why he thought sales had suddenly plummeted 15 percent. He immediately answered, "It's the wait time. Duh!"

"The wait time?" I asked.

"Our sales dropped when we increased the wait time on the phone from an average of three minutes to nearly nine minutes. They wanted to save money by having fewer inbound telemarketing agents."

Wow!

Further interviews proved the first stakeholder absolutely right. In fact, the data clearly showed that after the wait time went up, consumers simply hung up.

I asked the stakeholder why he hadn't shared this with his managers. His answer: "They never asked."

Point made.

What I frequently find is that most of my clients have a math problem: They can subtract but they can't add. They're extremely good at cost cutting, but they're not as good at increasing revenue. We know it's ten times more expensive to acquire a new customer than it is to keep an old one. It doesn't take a lot of math to realize that if customers leave because they're not being properly served, your company eventually fails. Too often, companies erroneously believe that if they reduce costs, they'll automatically make more money. They forget that customers have óptions, and an increase in wait time means people will go elsewhere. They assume the way to reach the low-hanging fruit is to reduce costs by reducing value, when the opposite is true. How does Apple justify having dozens of attendants in its stores when Best Buy has only a handful? Easily. Every attendant at Apple is selling something. If the stores had half the number of people, they'd sell half the amount of goods. Customers don't like to wait.

Leverage Participation with Best Practices

The best way to collaborate with your stakeholders is to bring in innovation best practices, several of which were discussed in Chapter 5. Innovation is a delicate ecosystem. You must create complete systems that include best practices that leverage socialization and game mechanics to drive the engagement necessary to make innovation really work. You want to create the opportunity for stakeholders to collaborate with each other by giving them a time and place to do it. Using social enterprise networks allows you to digitally engage stakeholders. Outside experts can set up the collaborative framework and provide the best practices so that you can execute it. It isn't expensive to implement, and the return on investment can be dramatic. War is waged on the battlefield of innovation, and that's where we'll win. Uber didn't reinvent taxicabs; Uber reinvented the way customers got from one place to another. This is disruptive innovation.

Impel Engagement via Internal Social Networks

One of the best ways to drive collaboration among stakeholders in an organization is to use enterprise social networks. These internal networks, similar to Facebook, allow you to post specific innovation challenges. I worked with a company that needed to significantly reduce operational costs in order to develop a product for its customers at a much lower price. The executives hosted an internal Biggest Loser Challenge and reached out to their 3,500 employees to find money leaks in their system. In just a few weeks, they had identified millions of dollars' worth of leaks and far surpassed their original goal of reducing operational costs. Using game mechanics and socialization, you can significantly increase stakeholder engagement and collaboration.

THE PARTNER COLLABORATIVE TYPE

Some of the best innovations come from the manner in which you create integrated value with strategic partners and alliances.

One of my clients is among the world's largest hospital chains. A goal of the chain was to improve the way in which it delivered safe clinical experiences to patients. To help achieve this goal, we conducted regular brainstorming sessions with several relevant vendors. What happened was astonishing.

In the exchange of ideas that ensued, we were able to come up with a range of new technologies and services. The cost to my client was zero, yet the estimated enterprise benefit was more than $15 million in reduced liability, increased patient throughput, and significantly improved patient satisfaction. Meanwhile, the vendor/partners increased their profits, opportunity, and involvement in the hospital. Not a bad outcome from just sitting down with partners and collaborating.

Partner relationships are extremely important strategic components to your overall customer experience success. In my own business, my strategic partners and alliances are critical to the way I deliver services to my clients.

THE COMPETITOR COLLABORATIVE TYPE

The term "open innovation" is widely used, but very few leaders understand its implications. From my perspective, open innovation means partnering with everyone—in some cases, even competitors.

One of the most interesting examples of open innovation can be found in Sierra Nevada Brewing Company, founded by Ken Grossman, a company I mentioned in Chapter 4. Ken believes that there actually are no competitors. He periodically collaborates with other brewers. For example, in honor of Sierra Nevada's thirtieth anniversary, he teamed up with four competitors who along with him had simultaneously spearheaded the craft beer trend, and they created a series of four beers, each brewed with a fellow craft beer pioneer. I think Ken's willingness to collaborate is a big part of his success and why he is so highly respected in the craft beer industry.

Most businesses have opportunities to collaborate with competitors in a way that delivers mutual benefit. These competitor collaborative types see the universe from the perspective of abundance. They don't fear collaboration and instead seek it out. They understand that collaboration with people in the same industry can add to greater mutual prosperity through an exchange of ideas, experiences, and skills.

Some competitors, however, see the universe from the perspective of scarcity. In other words, they see you as the enemy. Such competitors are not going to be good collaborative partners because they operate from a place of fear. So choose your competitor collaborations carefully, but certainly do not exclude this as part of your overall enterprise innovation commitment.

TAKEAWAYS

The most innovative companies have developed a culture of collaboration and cocreation. They develop technologies with a team that is encouraged to take smart risks in order to develop special products and services for their customers. They fuel this collaboration by encouraging courage.

The new concept of open innovation suggests that we can collaborate and cocreate even with competitors, but most important, we really need to take the time and effort to understand the customers we serve. We need to understand the hidden meaning and see the nuances that drive breakthrough customer experiences.

PART
TWO

MAPPING YOUR
CUSTOMER'S JOURNEY

I almost hate to use the term *journey mapping*, because the concept has been hijacked by so many people that it's become a generic term that doesn't mean much. The concept of looking at the way in which people experience the throughput of your product and brand—journey mapping—is something of a no-brainer. However, this simple concept has turned into a thousand-pound gorilla.

I'm a big fan of granularity when it comes to looking at what your customers love and hate across the big-picture touchpoints, but we need to be extremely careful that we don't evaluate touchpoints so minutely that the insights we gain are non-actionable.

In the early days of personal computing, you had to understand the cryptic code of the disk operating system (DOS), where you had to enter nonintuitive codes to get your computer to perform basic functions. In effect, the formula was: *complex and hard work in* → *simple computer functions out*. It wasn't until graphical user interface (GUI) arrived that personal computers exploded in popularity. GUI systems such as the Apple OS and Windows OS followed a new formula: *simple icon clicks* → *complex computer functions* → *simple computer functions out.*

In Part Two, I present five simple steps—the five touchpoints—that you can easily apply when mapping your customers' experience: the pre-touch, the first-touch, the core-touch, the last-touch, and the in-touch. Like GUI, it's that simple.

CHAPTER 7

THE PRE-TOUCHPOINT MOMENT

The pre-touch moment is the touchpoint that's not really a touchpoint. In its most simple form, it is when customers haven't yet engaged your product or service and are deciding if they want to give it a try. They're in the research phase.

For example, people may drive down the street and look at your restaurant to see if they're in for a great meal or ptomaine poisoning. Or they might search for you on their desktop or mobile device, bringing up Google, Yelp, and TripAdvisor ratings and reviews to find out your digital reputation among the highly influential community of existing and previous customers.

Most organizations have very little information about this all-important touchpoint primarily because it's hard to glean insights about a *potential* customer when there's been no point of contact. Whom do you ask and how do you make the connection? This is where social analytics is of enormous help.

Paradoxically, the main control you have over the pre-touch moment is found in the remaining four touchpoints. This is especially true digitally, involving your previous customers who interact and post reviews online assessing the quality of their experience with you. At the risk of sounding redundant, the key to the pre-touchpoint is to deliver amazing experiences across the other four touchpoints, digitally and non-digitally, across all of your customer types.

PLAY TO WIN: ENGENDER LOVE

In order to win at the pre-touchpoint, you must leverage the unbendable fact that we live in an information-sharing economy. It is hyper-connected and empowers your customers to promote you or destroy you.

If you're delivering customer service at the baseline level of expectation, then there's nothing for your customers to talk about. You have delivered an average experience, and they have no reason to even think about you again. If your customers are not talking about you, then you are not building your business. Your online presence is poor to nonexistent.

To get customers talking about you, you must deliver exceptional experiences across the other four touchpoints. This will make your customers want to rave about what a wonderful experience they had with you, which feeds the pre-touchpoint. Then, when prospective customers research you, they find that your customers love you.

The Zero Moment of Truth

The zero moment of truth (or ZMOT) is what Google calls the pre-touch information phase and the value created through delivering exceptional experiences to your customers. Your customers can conduct a complete background search on your business or product literally in seconds. If you are bad, there is no place to hide. If you are great, your customers will do your promoting for you.[1]

The good news is that if you deliver exceptional experiences, digitally and non-digitally, across all your customer types, you develop a digital and non-digital community reputation that will significantly improve sales while reducing customer acquisition costs.

It's great to know that we live in a universe where, when we serve others well, we are rewarded with happy workplaces, happy customers, and financial prosperity. Not a bad result for just paying attention to the customers we serve and deeply understanding what they love and what they hate.

Digital Ubiquity and Your Reputation

A well-known anecdote tells us that if you place a frog in hot water, it will leap to safety, but if you place it in cold water and then slowly heat the water, it will be boiled alive. In the second scenario, the frog presumably doesn't notice that the temperature is increasing and it sits calmly, blithely unaware that it's about to be boiled to death.

While scientifically this story is not true, it aptly demonstrates what happens when good companies don't pay attention to the changing environment. Many of these changes are gradual—for example, changes in your company's digital reputation. If you haven't caught on to the fact that your customers are talking to a whole lot of other people about their experiences with you, then you will suffer the fate of the frog and slowly be boiled to death.

Your digital reputation is the most important part of the pre-touch journey, as customers want to know if your product or service meets their needs. The digitally engaged customer community wants to know how you treat other customers. Digital equity is your best friend or your worst enemy. (Not all of your pre-touch moments are digital, but today most of them are.)

Digital connection is everywhere. The water has changed. Use it to thrive. Later in this chapter, I'll show you how with my Three-Step Pre-Touch Plan.

According to estimates, in 2021, more than one-quarter of the global population, or more than 3.8 billion people, use smartphones. The number of all mobile phone users is growing so fast it could exceed 7 billion by 2023.

Yet despite this massive sea change in the way people connect, an executive actually told me that the digital domain was irrelevant as it related to the way in which his company delivered customer experiences. Now that's a frog about to be boiled.

Add to this the advent and popularity of new wearable technologies, and it's clear that the way in which consumers connect will grow exponentially in importance. Organizations *and executives in digital denial will be left behind by the organizations that leverage this opportunity to deliver exquisite customer experiences.*

Non-Digital Perceptions and Your Reputation

I've spent a lot of time talking about your customer's digital pre-touch experience. The fact is, most of your customers experience you digitally prior to engaging you physically. It doesn't matter if you are a donut shop or a multibillion-dollar business-to-business enterprise, because the same rules apply: you're going to get Googled. Full stop.

However, for many businesses, there is also a non-digital pre-touchpoint. If you are a local donut shop located on the main street of your town (or an In-N-Out Burger, as discussed in Chapter 4), your most important pre-touch moment might very well be the physical appearance of your business: the parking lot, your sign, the landscaping, what people see when they look into your windows, and all the other aspects of what customers might expect if they were to do business with you.

Apple is one of the largest and most successful companies on Earth. Have you been to an Apple store lately? They're the epitome of cool and hip, just like Apple products. The size of your company doesn't matter or whether you sell donuts, iPhones, or something in between, but if you have a physical place where customers come to check you out, make sure you don't let them down. It's as simple as that. If you have a shabby sign and landscaping and if your interior isn't clean and wow-looking, then you will bite it digitally when you are reviewed.

In order to understand how to build the perfect pre-touch moment, you need to get out of your chair and do research—to listen and observe strategically. Drive down the street and envision how customers might perceive the quality of your food and/or experience based on what they see. Walk around your building and peer through the windows as if you were a potential customer. What do you see, hear, smell, and think?

In order to succeed in developing the perfect pre-touch moment, you need to understand that you are delivering both digitally and non-digitally. Although some businesses are far more digital than others, it's important that you research both aspects to make sure that you are providing an integrated quality experience.

> *"Quality is more important than quantity.*
> *One home run is much better than two doubles."*
> —STEVE JOBS

When You're Great, You Have Nothing to Hide

It's amazing how much work companies put into trying to push down derogatory business ratings. However, people are smart. Ultimately, your potential customers will find out who has been naughty and who has been nice.

If you deliver exceptional experiences, your customer community will share the good news digitally. They will become your best source of advertising. Regrettably, however, customers are far more likely to post derogatory information about your business, and that's why digital reputations tend to skew negative.

The only way to solve this is by being really, really *good*. Will some nutcase say something bad about you anyway? Yes, of course, but what I have found is that your real customer community typically neutralizes negative comments, especially if those comments are wrong or false.

THE THREE-STEP PRE-TOUCH PLAN

If you follow the steps in my pre-touch plan, you not only won't boil in the changing water temperatures of the fast-paced world but you'll be able to use the changes to your advantage and help current customers get you more customers.

Step 1:
Do the Research

The first step in designing the perfect pre-touch moment is to understand what your customers are already experiencing at this key touchpoint. You must conduct comprehensive digital and non-digital research on what your prospective customers experience when they look at your business or organization.

It's surprising to me how few organizations take time away from their internal focus to actually think about the way people see their business, especially when this simple step can reveal huge inadequacies and surprising positives that you otherwise wouldn't know about. It doesn't take long and is massively worth the effort.

T*he other day I was at a popular restaurant in California. I noticed behind the counter a hospital can of bug spray,* *and I instantly thought, "My God, this place is infested with bugs! I'm outta here!" So I left. Superficial analysis? Maybe, but customers do see us superficially. If we're not mindful of this, we can make big mistakes that have long-term consequences for our organization.*

Step 2:
Invent

Many find the words *invent* and *innovate* lofty. They might bring up schoolroom memories of Thomas Edison or Henry Ford. I believe, though, that the best innovations of the future will not be about products but will be more about business model changes and the way in which we serve customers.

Everyone is an inventor, so don't let the idea intimidate you. Your goal is to gain insights about what your customers hate and what they love so you can create layered and dynamic value. Start from this angle and your innovations will make doing business with you much more worthwhile than doing business with your competitors.

In many ways, humans are superficial in how we initially decide what we like and what we hate. For example, we might judge a person's intelligence by their vocabulary, yet vocabulary rarely is an indication of real intelligence. We judge products by their package design, yet there is no direct correlation between a great package and a great product.

Based on this, some might suggest that image is more important than actual quality, but they would be wrong. Every single touchpoint tells the story of the quality, sophistication, and ultimately value of your product or service. Therefore, in the superficial world we live in, you need to be judicious and surgical about how you create every single component and experience no matter how irrelevant they may seem.

Step 3:
Hardwire Customer Insights

What customers like and what they hate changes every day. You need to develop a range of systems and processes to monitor both digital and non-digital customer experiences, so that you continually increase incremental and breakthrough customer innovations.

Following is a checklist of ideas you can use to continually improve your customers' experience by gaining better insights.

Insight and Innovation Checklist

❑ **Google Alerts.** If you're in a smaller organization without a big social analytic budget, set up Google Alerts on keywords that are relevant to your business name, industry, and competition. It's easy to do—just Google it. Alerts can keep you in the loop on industry news.

❏ **Social Analytics.** If you're in a larger organization, use social analytics to monitor keyword themes. This can help you understand the dialogue around your industry and competition as well as your specific business.

❏ **Walk About.** It's amazing how few executives get out of their corner office to experience their business across all touchpoints through their customers' eyes. But some of the best organizations in the world routinely place top executives in frontline positions so they can see firsthand what their organizational policies look like when they are delivered to the customer. This shouldn't be a once-in-a-lifetime experience. Rather, it should be done weekly. Start with the commonsense approach of "walking a mile in your customers' shoes."

❏ **Insight Challenges.** Create a challenge for stakeholders that offers incentives for ideas on how to improve the customer experience. (This is similar to the challenge for your customers that we discussed in Chapter 6.) I use this approach in my consulting practice with tremendous success. Although digitizing the challenge isn't required, the process works best when used within enterprise social networks or an internal social platform. Insight challenges are amazing, inexpensive, and work every time.

recently worked with a large hospital chain where we created the "What Patients Hate Challenge." We discovered that patients hated sitting with other sick people in *the waiting room for forty-five minutes before seeing the doctor. Surprise, surprise!*

Nobody had ever asked the patients what they hated. Unfortunately, this is common across all industry categories. For some reason, we don't ask the people actually affected: our customers. Once we understand what our customers hate, we can usually fix it. So we created a patient throughput plan that virtually eliminated any waiting. As a result, we increased customer satisfaction and profitability. For the same hospital chain we also successfully created a "What Patients Love Challenge" so we could find ways to deliver more of the same.

❏ **Insight Champions.** Some of the best organizations hire "chief listening officers" or appoint "insight champions." Their express purpose is to get timely and meaningful insights about customers' loves and hates. Every business should have the equivalent of an insight champion who can report to top leaders on opportunities to design better experiences.

VOODOO AND THE IPHONE BOX

Recently, I surveyed customers who had bought a new iPhone, and I had some fascinating insights. Amazingly, 80 percent of the customers kept the box the phone came in for more than three months after their purchase. What kind of voodoo magic does

Apple have over these intelligent people? What would make them keep their iPhone box? More important, why should you or I care about the answer?

You could easily argue that the iPhone box is nothing more than the package the product came in. You already decided to buy the phone before you ever experience its box.

The fact is that the box is important because Apple's tremendous success boils down to one simple concept: Apple understands that it's in the business of *human experience*. Every single touchpoint at an Apple retailer and with the Apple product is exquisite. There are no interruptions in the continuum of great experiences. Apple provides a holistic, incredible experience at all touchpoints, and this includes the box in which the product arrives.

I've heard some people describe the iPhone box as if it were a Fabergé egg because it's just that beautiful. And the voodoo doesn't stop at its looks. The big surprise when you open the box isn't what you get—it's what you *don't* get: warranty cards, instruction booklets in nine different languages, cross-marketing material, and other propaganda that no one wants.

You don't need the instruction manual because the product is designed to work intuitively and there are no error codes because the product itself is nonproblematic. Apple doesn't cross-market because the company delivers an exceptional product that makes you want to buy its other products. The moral: what appears to be simple and almost accidental is the product of tremendous research and thought. For this reason, Apple made something as superficial as a box absolutely delicious.

GETTING THE PRE-TOUCH MOMENT RIGHT

All industries, companies, and cultures are unique. Your pre-touch plan needs to be customized in a way that fits the distinctiveness of your organization. When you apply this simple concept of a tailored pre-touch moment both digitally and non-digitally, it has an amazing impact on the success of your business.

As you formalize this process and hardwire it to your organization's behaviors, you will begin to lead your industry in customer satisfaction and loyalty.

TAKEAWAYS

One of the biggest problems with the pre-touchpoint is that much of the customer contact is behind the scenes. It's the point at which your customer is vetting you, looking at social networks, and researching you, your product, and your service on platforms such as Google and YouTube. Because this is happening without your knowledge, it's sometimes hard to intervene.

The best way to have a good pre-touch experience for your potential customers is to deliver free and valuable resources prior to their commitment to buying your product or service. Get them to love you first, and then they'll come to you of their own choice and volition.

Remember, too, that if you are not delivering exceptional experiences across your other touchpoints, the research your consumers unearth will be negative. Billions of dollars are deflected away from companies because customers have done their research and decided not to do business with them. As I've said before, it's impossible not to have the odd irrational customer who hates you for no real reason; nevertheless, most derogatory comments on influential social networks and other digitally visible directories contain some grain of truth. The issues could have been resolved had the company put the time and effort into building an integrated customer experience plan.

The sad truth is, each month, dozens, hundreds, or maybe thousands of customers are researching companies like yours and deciding not to do business with them based on what they discover. Don't let this happen to you!

CHAPTER 8

THE FIRST TOUCHPOINT MOMENT

As individuals, most of us are aware of the importance of making a good first impression, and we're generally pretty good about it. Organizations, on the other hand, often fail miserably at this. They don't understand that the first touchpoint is crucial. It is the point at which we have the greatest opportunity to create the trajectory for the rest of our relationship with the customer. In fact, if we fail at the first touchpoint, it is extremely problematic and ultimately expensive to fix the resulting damage. For this reason, it is essential to get it right from the beginning.

The first touchpoint occurs when your customers engage you and your brand, digitally, non-digitally, or sometimes both. They have done their research and they're making initial contact; they haven't bought anything yet. They might be speaking to a customer service representative or entering your shop and breathing in the scent of your business. If it's a digital first-touch, they might be filling out the contact form on your website, reading your blog, or preparing to call the phone number listed on your website.

I called a prospective vendor the other day. On my first try, the phone rang twelve times before I finally hung up. The second time I called, I reached a surly representative. You can be sure I will never do business with that vendor.

Never neglect your first touchpoint.

Imagine walking into a dentist's office for your first visit. It's the first time you've gone to that dentist, with whom you hope to create a long-term relationship. As you enter, you hear in the background the sound of the dentist's drill and someone moaning. As you approach the front desk, the receptionist there is arguing with a patient about a missed payment. Dentist visits can be upsetting, but these poor first touchpoints make them more so. The walls between the treatment rooms and the reception area should have been insulated. The receptionist might have taken the patient to a private area to discuss the payment, or if this was not possible, could have spoken softly. In general, a receptionist should always be friendly and engaging and make sure you are comfortable as you wait for your turn to see the dentist. Soothing music and an aquarium in the waiting area also help ease the anxiety of waiting patients.

What business owners often don't realize is that as customers engage you, they are hit with a barrage of multisensory experiences. In many ways, it's the totality of these fast-firing micro-experiences that equals the first-touch. First touchpoints have multiple moving parts, and they all need to be aligned. And the closer the customer gets to the core value proposition—a pain-free and stress-free dentist's visit, for example—the more important these experiences become. Remember, your mission statement expresses your core value statement. The closer the customer gets to the core experience you offer (see Chapter 9), the more closely aligned that experience must be to your mission statement. Every step along the way is important. So, although a certain amount of trust was established at the pre-touch moment, it can easily be destroyed by a sloppy first-touch experience.

Exceptional organizations are extremely judicious about designing layered and dynamic experiences at the first touchpoint. Dutch Bros. is an amazing drive-through coffee kiosk. While there are any number of drive-through coffee stands that serve reasonably good coffee, Dutch Bros. stands apart because it does an amazing job of connecting with its customers. Employees are trained to engage the customers. They ask how your day is going and then try to make a connection with you beyond the superficial by opening authentic conversations. The purpose is to create a positive experience that goes far beyond great coffee at a great price.

I recently went to my local Dutch Bros. I had not been there for more than a month, yet the attendant remembered my name and even what we had talked about. (I, on the other hand, have a hard time remembering what I had for breakfast.) Every time I visit the local kiosk, the relationship gets better.

YOUR BRAIN AND THE FIRST-TOUCH MOMENT

The human brain functions on both a conscious and subconscious level. We develop powerful and in some cases permanent opinions of people, brands, and businesses, and often these opinions are created without us even knowing it.

At the non-digital first touchpoint, customers' brains rapidly absorb the smells, sounds, tastes, and sights of that encounter. Ask yourself, "Is my store or restaurant welcoming and filled with exceptional sensory details?" At the digital first touchpoint, customers take in the design, color, and sometimes music that might be playing on your website or blog. Ask yourself: "Is my site welcoming and are customers easily able to find the information they're looking for?"

First touchpoints can be subtle or obvious. The subtle messages you send during the first touchpoint, and which you may think are harmless, will accumulate, even if subconsciously, in your customers' brains. So examine your first touchpoint very carefully.

Unpleasant first touchpoints can also be blaringly obvious. There is a restaurant not far from where I live that serves truly excellent food and provides great service. However, the temperature in the restaurant is always freezing cold. Although we love the food, we rarely go there because sitting in the subarctic temperature is just too uncomfortable.

Never underestimate the permanent impact of your first touchpoints on the customer experience.

The net customer experience is the difference between what the customer expects and what the customer gets. Companies that deliver experiences below customers' expectations post a net loss, while those that deliver experiences above expectations see a net gain.

The Non-Digital First-Touch

The first touchpoint experiences bombard your customers. As they pull into your driveway, the sensory stream begins. They begin to form an opinion based on the cleanliness of your parking lot and the physical appearance of your building. They analyze the convenience of the parking as they walk to the door. Once they enter, they assess the smell, the sounds, the temperature, and many other subliminal and less conspicuous data points. All of these sensory inputs begin the process of customers forming a heavily weighted initial opinion. This is the first-touch experience.

Let's say you have a fast-food restaurant. As customers get closer and closer to their goal of buying and eating your hamburger, the importance of the smells, sounds, and appearance increases. It culminates with their first contact with the staff. Do the workers smile as the customers approach? Are they and their uniforms clean? Is the counter clean? Do the workers get the order right? Are they happy, or do they seem to be working reluctantly? Remember the Net Customer Value Strata (Chapter 3) when you're thinking about designing your first touchpoint. Your non-digital first touchpoint should be outrageously good to compete in the hyper-competitive marketplace.

This Just Got Personal: When I was researching fast-food restaurants, I found that the most popular ones quickly got personal. In great restaurants like In-N-Out Burger, as you pull up to the drive-through or approach the counter, you are greeted with a sincere smile and often asked how your day is going. This instantly changes the relationship from transactional to personal. As your neurons continue firing, you ingest the subtleties of the highly trained experts behind the counter.

The heavily weighted first touchpoint is so perfectly deployed at great businesses that you may not even consciously notice the signals the staff is sending your way. What you do know is that a friendly person is looking you in the eyes and engaging you in a way that creates a connection. As you design the perfect customer journey, remember that this personal connection is the perfect launchpad for an exceptional journey.

Failure to Launch: The flip side of an *exceptional* non-digital first-touch moment is, of course, a *bad* first-touch moment. For example, have you ever been greeted at an airport ticket counter by an employee determined to make you suffer?

It's incredible how many organizations have disconnected from their customers and the stakeholders who connect with their customers, and they are clueless about why they're losing ground. Many businesses' customer encounters are, at their very best, only at the baseline of customer expectation. Many more—perhaps most—are far below customers' expectations. Much of this has to do with the first touchpoint.

If you blow the first touchpoint, you will have an expensive and difficult time bringing that customer back. Moreover, that customer is going to share their experience, destroy your reputation, and begin the process of killing your business. Does that sound overly dramatic? It's not. I've seen this happen hundreds of times, and I've learned that it is so much easier to prevent this from happening than to try to fix it later.

The Digital First-Touch

Recently, I bought my daughter a food processor to take with her to college. Of course, my pre-touch meant going to Amazon and doing research. I learned that customers rated one brand higher than others. I read the customers' posts and saw how many people rated the product. This is important because the greater the pool of reviewers, the more accurate the overall rating. This is pre-touch, and Amazon does it well.

The first-touch was the moment when I decided to buy the product, but *before* I clicked and actually became a customer (the core touchpoint). At this first touchpoint, Amazon engaged me with relevant offers. Based on what I was viewing, Amazon showed me other food processors as alternatives—maybe cheaper, maybe more advanced, maybe a newer release. The company offered free shipping and accessories (like storage covers and additional blades) based on what other customers had bought. All of it was relevant. Amazon wasn't insulting me with offers for shoes or car parts. The company knew what I was looking for and provided highly pertinent information based on what other people looking for the same thing had purchased.

CAVEAT EMPTOR:
TOO IMPORTANT NOT TO BE TAKEN SERIOUSLY

A national electronics retailer misses opportunities to create exceptional first-touch experiences by stationing a security guard at the entrance. While this might help prevent theft, it's a lousy way to greet your customers and is a classic example of a misused first touchpoint. If you're like me, you want to be loved and trusted, and I assume everyone feels this way.

At the other end of the spectrum, the first touchpoint at an Apple retail store is entirely different. Instead of being greeted by a security guard, you are attended by friendly Apple-evangelists who know and love the product. They politely probe to find out who you are and what you love and hate, and they deliver a well-thought-out, beautiful experience. Apple understands that customers don't want to feel distrusted. Instead, they want specific experiences that are both relevant and exceptional.

Just like the incredible attention to design the company puts into its minimalistic packaging, Apple mindfully designs its first touchpoints. Apple's retail environments are open, nonthreatening, and by most customers' accounts, delicious.

Apple got its start by taking complexity out of personal computers. The company designed the Macintosh in a way that was easy to understand, with highly engaging icons that made it easy to use. The secret to Apple's success in retail is much the same: the ability to translate simplicity and design into a beautiful human experience in a retail setting.

The takeaway: although we need to deliver exceptional and holistic experiences at every touchpoint, the first touchpoint is turbocharged. The good news is that many organizations—some of which might be your competition—design these heavily weighted experiences haphazardly. They give no more thought to the first-touch than they do to any other customer journey touchpoint. This is where you can gain a competitive advantage by delivering a truly exceptional first touchpoint.

Think about how the first touchpoints below might affect a customer. Remember, at this point, the customer has already done research and decided to consider using the company's product or service. Now put yourself in the customer's shoes and imagine, for example:

- What you see as you walk into a new dentist's office.

- The smells and sights as you walk into a restaurant for the first time.

- The greeting you receive as you approach the reception counter at a hotel.

- The first few words you hear as you listen to a keynote speaker.

- The flight attendant's greeting as you board an airplane.

Now consider these first touchpoints as they relate to your organization:

- What visitors see when landing on your website.

- The quality of the free value you deliver on your website and whether it is meaningful.

- How easy it is to get what you want from your digital resources.

- How your graphic images communicate your quality and value.

All of these powerful first touchpoints can communicate a story of value, quality, and excellence. However, many organizations communicate an ill-thought-out set of human experiences that are incomplete or flawed.

The first touchpoint is where the low-hanging fruit is, yet most businesses pay little attention to these experiences. As a result, they are under-invented and unimaginative, which leads to mediocre customer experiences. By paying careful attention to your first-touch moments, you can outperform the competition.

A colleague suggested I reach out to a firm he uses for some of his business development activities. Because this is such an important part of any organization's activities, you need to be cautious in selecting a business development vendor. Since this firm had been recommended by a friend, though, it had overcome any initial suspicions I may have had about the company's skill sets and professionalism.

I decided to call. An automated receptionist answered and gave me a dozen or so confusing options. Finally, frustrated, I selected "O" for the operator to leave a message in the general voicemail. Four days later, I still hadn't heard from the firm, so I called and again found myself in a digital maze. This time, however, I left a message in the CEO's voicemail explaining I'd called before and hadn't received a call back.

A week passed without a reply. I was now completely over the firm. There is literally nothing the company could do to ever win my business. Its people had had two opportunities to engage me, and they failed miserably.

The moral of the story is that poor first touchpoints can kill your business forever. You must pay attention to these highly important digital and non-digital moments.

DESIGNING FIRST TOUCHPOINTS FOR ALL YOUR CUSTOMER TYPES

Some companies have a very narrow set of customer types. For example, I recently did some work for Freightliner, a great, well-run company that manufactures trucks. Freightliner dealers all serve a similar customer type: truck drivers. Although not identical, truck drivers have many common success characteristics, which makes it easy for dealers to design relevant and exceptional experiences for this very narrow customer type.

Conversely, businesses that sell to macro markets need to do significantly more heavy lifting to identify the range of their customer types to be certain they deliver exceptional human experiences to their customers. Amazon, for example, appeals to all kinds of customer types. The company understands what people universally care about, so its interface is easy to use. After that, Amazon appeals to different buyer types—for example, the price conscious, the transactional, the analytical, and those interested in the highest quality. In this way, the company addresses everyone. It also allows for social ratings and comparative price points and provides remarkable visual detail.

The range of your customer types affects how you manage your first touchpoint. Once again, we circle back to your types in order to make sure each finds an exceptional experience at that first point of contact. For some companies, like Freightliner, this is easy. For others with a wide range of customer types, like Amazon, it takes more work and creativity. Whatever your customer type range, this first contact is full of opportunity—for success and failure.

You Can't Spend Your Way to Exceptional

Not long ago, I began working with a company that was spending millions of dollars a year to gain consumer insights. Data was gleaned from every possible big data source you can imagine. The company was willing to spend a great deal of money to gain this information, because it rightly assumed this could drive the best customer innovations.

However, after a one-week audit of the data, I realized something shocking. I could not find one piece connecting the insights the company paid for to any *actionable innovations that delivered improved customer value*. We fixed that problem by ensuring the company evaluated the data it was collecting, turned that data into information, and then took action where it could get a measurable return on investment.

Unfortunately, this isn't an isolated incident. I believe it is now commonplace for organizations to pay for consumer insights they have no system for or way to use. Typically, when I conduct a customer insights audit, I find thousands of pages of graphs and charts. While sometimes bits of information are actually useful, most often there's little of value. But the bigger problem is that even when the data is useful, the company has no way to make the insights actionable. The personnel don't know, or haven't bothered to learn, how to transmute the information into something that delivers real value to the customer and the market.

I believe the best way to gain great insights at all customer journey touchpoints is for businesses to get closer to their customers to find out what they really care about. By navigating to where your customers are and observing what they love and hate, you will be able to design amazing experiences that matter and execute them like a ninja.

How to Create the Perfect First-Touch Moment

Good insights are the key to any successful innovation. In order to build out great customer value across the customer journey, you must find out what they hate and what they love. Below are some simple questions that can have an enormous impact when you shape your first touchpoints. Ask yourself:

- Have I identified the various components that make up the first touchpoints across all my customer types?

- Have I set up listening posts digitally and non-digitally to gain the kinds of insights I need to invent a better experience?

- Do I conduct weekly or monthly brainstorming sessions where I invite customer-facing, frontline employees to present ideas on how to improve first touchpoints?

- Have I developed an incentive or rewards program for the best ideas on how to improve the customer experience across various touchpoints?

- Do I use social and other digital analytic tools to gain insights about what my customer types hate and love about the range of products and services I provide?

- Have I developed vendor and customer innovation groups to help come up with better ideas on how to uniquely serve my valued customers?

Dig Deeper:
Go Granular

My goal is to provide you with an easy-to-understand roadmap that is actionable for both large and small companies. For this reason, I broke down the various customer touchpoints into five easy-to-understand moments. As you become more skilled at building the perfect customer experience, you will want to become more granular.

For example, if you own a burrito stand in Los Angeles, you may want to start by asking yourself if your signage is clear so potential customers driving by can easily find you. You may ask yourself how simple or secure it is for customers to park. You would likely want to ask yourself what's going through the heads of your customers as they approach your business; how you communicate quality, cleanliness, and the deliciousness of your burritos; what the expressions on the faces of the counter staff convey; and if the aroma of your burritos wafting through the window is enticing. All of these elements are part of the first touchpoint.

Next, break these down into more granular components, so as to make an amazing totality. A word of warning: don't become so granular that you turn this into a doctoral thesis. You just want to make sure you're not missing anything as you dissect the touchpoint. Loves and hates are relative; they come in degrees. Some people aren't bothered by standing in line; other people abhor it. Some live and die for a great burrito; others can take them or leave them. Understand these gradations and how granular you need to be. It would be too granular, for example, if a fast-food restaurant had its front counter people keep track of how many customers of different age groups, ethnicities, and hair color come into the restaurant. At the end of the day, the data you accumulate should lead to innovating better customer experiences, not create complexity and inertia. When you design your customer experiences, make sure the process is both complete and customized to your customer types and your business culture.

In this age of big data, we assume more is better. I worked for a client that actually had a data war room where the team would examine its customer database, which included sometimes erroneous and certainly irrelevant small data points, to microscopic levels of granular detail. The competition was ahead of them simply because they offered better products and service. Understand what data you need, then acquire and aggregate it. The best way to know if you're at the right level of granularity is if you end up delivering more customer and business value than the resources required to accumulate and assess your data.

TAKEAWAYS

Two things will determine whether or not your design of the perfect first-touch moment is successful:

1. The experience must be **complete**. You need to deliver wonderful experiences across each of the five distinct customer touchpoints in both digital and non-digital channels, and you have to do it across the entire range of customer types. Most organizations succeed at doing just one of these, and as a result, the competition destroys them.

2. The experience must be **designed** in a way that's customized for your customer types and fits the culture of your business.

It is essential that you focus on making sure your first-touch moment is flawless so you don't have to spend an inordinate amount of time and money trying to fix it later. If you start off on the wrong foot with customers, in most cases, you never win them back. Even if you do, it will be at great expense and pain.

CHAPTER 9

THE CORE TOUCHPOINT MOMENT

The core touchpoint experience occurs when customers are engaging with your product, brand, or service. By the time customers reach this point, they would already have navigated the research phase of the pre-touch and initial engagement of the first touchpoint moments.

Too many organizations focus *only* on the core touchpoint, and regrettably, they tend to do it in a way that doesn't deliver exceptional experiences. Instead, they are inconsistent at this touchpoint, and the result is unreliable, variable, and fractionated customer experiences. In the old days, companies could succeed even if they delivered these mediocre experiences, but today such experiences guarantee business failure.

Organizations often emphasize the core touchpoint but do not always apply it consistently. It's important that you do so and also that you make certain that it fits comfortably with the other touchpoint experiences you create along your customers' journey.

The core experience itself is really a series of internal touchpoints. For example, let's assume you've done your research and decided to try a new restaurant. You arrive and the gracious hostess seats you at a beautiful table with a view of the water. Once you've been seated, you continue to have core touchpoint experiences. Your server greets you, another staff member pours your water, and the sommelier offers to help you with your wine selection. It's all going beautifully until you visit the restroom, which is disgusting. Because it isn't clean, you assume the restaurant has cleanliness problems everywhere, and your dinner is ruined. One poor core touchpoint can unravel everything positive in the customer experience.

SELF-ANALYSIS:
WHAT DOING BUSINESS WITH YOU IS LIKE

As a management consultant, I'm frequently shocked at how many companies have never asked themselves, *What is it like to do business with us?* In taking executives through this self-scrutiny, I often discover the reason they haven't is that they are ashamed of the services and experiences they provide. As you build out your core experience, sit down with your team and really ask, "What is it like to do business with us?" Be honest, get outside input, and most important, *act on* the insights you glean from this process.

Most organizations transition through a corporate or enterprise life cycle. In the beginning, they are market- and customer-focused. As time marches on, if they are successful, they begin to turn inward and operationalize their business; in other words, they start to spend way more time on the internal functions of the business than on their external customer. At one level, this makes good sense. For example, if you're a sandwich shop and you make the best sandwiches on the planet, you get really, really busy. Now, not only are you making these amazing sandwiches, but you're also trying to find ways to increase your customer flow; you're addressing issues related to parking, you're hiring more people so you need to build up your human resources infrastructure, and so on.

Unfortunately, at this point, as most organizations transition from being **customer-centric** to **operations-centric**, they go into hyper-internal focus. This is like a turtle going into its shell. Instead of looking outward, they concentrate on internal issues like managing staff, rules and regulations, shipping, and the supply chain. These are all important functions that serve the company, but they have little direct effect on customer value. It's a natural cycle and one to watch out for because it can cause companies to pretty much shut off any external listening and connection to the customer. Unfortunately, in today's world, this approach is almost a guarantee of failure because what is critical to success is a customer-centric culture that delivers exceptional experiences across the entire customer journey.

The Profit and Protection Myth

A common pitfall as companies slide into internal focus is that they begin to model their business, and therefore their core experiences, on "profit and protection." More attention is paid to how profits can be gained than to how customer experiences can be made exceptional. Inevitably, customer interactions sour. Then, instead of understanding this as a symptom of being too internally focused, the organization quickly builds out customer-punitive policies to protect itself from the very customers it is in business to serve.

If you sample a hundred retail or storefront businesses that have been in existence for more than ten years, the chances are high that each has experienced some sort of litigation over any of a wide range of things, not the least of which is a person's slipping and falling on the premises. Being sued is an emotional and traumatic experience, and the natural reaction is to protect oneself. However, businesses commonly go into an overprotective mode.

Take our fictional NeoWash car wash as an example. During a car wash, a windshield wiper snaps off. If NeoWash had customer-punitive policies to protect itself, these might include having customers sign a windshield wiper release form. But customers are busy people, and asking them to sign a form would take time. Moreover, it would also set a bad tone for the rest of the experience. Instead, the owner of NeoWash could think of broken windshield wipers as a cost of doing business and include replacement windshield wipers in the annual budget. Employees could be trained to be appropriately sorry if wipers break, but at the same time immediately and pleasantly offer to replace the wipers at no cost. Be customer-centric and win every time.

Unfortunately, new organizational profit mandates add to the shift away from a customer-centric focus to a profit-centric enterprise focus. When they occur alongside customer-punitive policies, it is a recipe for a toxic culture of contempt for the customer.

Y ou may have noticed over the past several years that many major retailers have lightened up on their returns policies. In the beginning, a few major retailers made it easy to return products; then, just to stay in the game, other retailers were obliged to follow suit. Retailers that continue to use punitive return policies will find themselves irrelevant in today's customer-driven economy. They are building policies that punish the customer in order to protect their profits.

Spank Your Customers and They Will Spank You Back

One of the biggest causes of customer experience failure, especially in midsize to large organizations, is an incessant focus on regulatory compliance and risk management. At one level, this is understandable. Businesses have a right to implement systems to protect themselves. What's wrong is the nonstop daily focus on it. Race car drivers have a saying, "Never look at the wall," which is smart because if you do, that's where you're going to go.

Organizations that set their sights internally place their backs to the customer. Healthcare, for example, doesn't have any oxygen left after all the regulation and compliance management. There are reams of policies and procedures, most of which routinely punish the customers healthcare organizations serve. You can't look at customers as something that needs to be managed, risk-wise. A company's biggest risk isn't lawsuits—it's that no one shows up.

R egulatory compliance and risk management are no longer excuses for delivering poor service.

Highly regulated industries like finance and banking have created systems and methods to protect themselves that go far beyond what's required and ultimately inconvenience their customers. Look at your industry's rules and find ways to serve your customers despite these requirements. If you don't, disgruntled customers will leave you—and will let other people know of their poor experience—for the disruptive innovators out there who have invented exceptional experiences to replace yours.

In other words, if you spank your customers, they will spank you back with a bad online review as they sashay out the door to your competitor. Does this mean that your organization doesn't have a responsibility to comply with regulations and use reasonable processes to manage risk? No! But you have to stop taking a myopic organization-centric view if you want to connect to your customers.

I t turns out that the biggest risk to organizations isn't managing operational risk. It's actually the risk of bankruptcy that results from destroying your business's customer relationships.

This hyper-focus on risk management happens all too often. The cycle is familiar and enormously destructive. To succeed in today's market, you must have a customer-centric business model, not an enterprise-driven one. Organizations need to be on the lookout for and constantly guard against falling into an organization-centric mode to prevent this cycle from happening. Like a freight train, once you damage your culture by putting your customer second, it's hard to turn it around. Perhaps more important, influential networks, public rating systems, and the entire digital grid will not forget or forgive your bad behavior.

A friend of mine always dreamed of opening an organic fruit and vegetable stand. After he retired, he opened his store, which was a huge success. His business grew like crazy and expanded and expanded.

One day, a woman in high heels slipped on some grapes that had fallen into the aisle. She went sailing across the room, landing square on her derrière. She did what every American does: she sued. From then on, my friend went into grape management mode. He posted signs, he allowed no one without rubber-soled shoes in the grape aisle, and he banned high heels everywhere in the store. It got to the point where the entire flow of his business had changed. His customers resented the new policies and stopped coming.

Worse, it killed his spirit. He went from viewing his customers as people who shared his love and passion for organic food to seeing them all as plaintiffs. He overreacted to cover his rear, and in the process, he created policies and behaviors that disconnected him from his business and customers.

The rational solution? Keep your store clean and safe, and get a good liability insurance policy. Then welcome your valued customers with a smile.

Businesses must resist the temptation to create an infrastructure that punishes all customers to fix a problem caused by 1 percent of their customers. Too often, companies build punitive policies that create distance between the customer and the company. Recently, some businesses have even taken to filing lawsuits against online reviewers who give them bad ratings. They don't realize that not having customers who love them is their single biggest risk in our hyper-connected, hyper-consumer-focused economy.

Liability vs. Customer-Friendly Policies: Many organizations have convinced themselves that they cannot build customer-friendly business practices that also manage liability and regulatory compliance. Unfortunately, this false and lazy belief leads to an adversarial relationship between the company and customer. As the saying goes, it's easy to default to the easy.

Successful organizations, on the other hand, know that regulatory compliance and risk management is required, but they use innovation and creativity to drive both customer experience and risk management concurrently. It takes time, effort, and a willingness to risk new ideas, but the results are a successful, client-focused business. Below I show you how to do it.

The idea that it is mutually exclusive to manage risk while managing perfect customer experiences is a well-propagated and destructive myth.

FOSTERING TRUST WITHIN THE CORE

In retail trades, one of the biggest problems is theft—also known as shrinkage—and over the years organizations have deployed many technologies and processes to control it.

According to the National Association for Shoplifting Prevention, there are more than 27 million habitual shoplifters, or one in eleven Americans, in the United States today.

The owners of a Northern California grocery chain take a unique approach to the problem of theft because they know that designing core experiences that communicate trust is critical to building a business that excels and lasts. Like Walmart, they position a greeter at the front door who welcomes shoppers and gives them a shopping cart. Little do the shoppers realize that the greeter is actually a security guard. Because of the way it is presented, the core experience is positive; it does not in any way suggest that the store doesn't trust its customers.

By using creative approaches, we can address business best practices while simultaneously delivering exceptional experiences that respect the customers we serve.

PUNITIVE POLICIES KILL BUSINESSES

I consult for an organization that manages resorts. The executives reached out to me because they'd experienced a significant drop in reservations, despite representing some of the best hotels in California.

After an analysis of their online booking and inbound telemarketing processes, we found a simple problem: they had changed their cancellation policy from twenty-four to seventy-two hours' notice. Their customers had many options for getaways and often made advance reservations that they canceled at the last minute if they decided to go elsewhere. The organization's new cancellation policy forced customers to make their decision sooner, which didn't sit well with the customers who bailed.

The policy made perfect sense to the company executives because it eliminated last-minute cancellations. But by trying to protect themselves with a policy that customers considered punitive, the executives ended up with customers punishing them by not booking at all. Today's empowered customers simply found better options.

I did the math to demonstrate the cost of customer acquisition versus the cost of keeping current customers. The executives instantly realized that any advantage provided by the new cancellation policy was reversed by the cost of acquiring new customers. Plus, how many potential new customers would avoid them simply because people shared their stories via social media?

Punitive policies like this demonstrate a complete lack of innovation because virtually all such policies could be reinvented to create a win-win scenario. Most organizations have a bucket of punitive policies they don't even recognize are punitive. How about yours? In our customer-driven economy, where customers are presented with unlimited choices and a quick and easy way to determine which choice is best, it is time for you to rethink any of your business's policies that aren't customer-friendly. Take a close look. Do an honest assessment and see how you unintentionally might be destroying your customers' exceptional core experience.

MAKE AN UPSET CUSTOMER A LIFELONG CUSTOMER IN FIVE EASY STEPS

No matter the business, eventually you're going to have an upset customer. So what should you do to reduce or eliminate the conflict? Over the last three decades, I've developed a simple plan to turn every upset customer into a customer for life. Remember, in our connected economy, ignoring an unhappy customer is a bad idea. Statistics show that upset customers are far more likely to share their bad experience on social and digital networks than happy customers, and the impact of negative reviews can be catastrophic. For many businesses, going from a 5-star Yelp rating to a 4-star rating can directly result in 10 to 20 percent reductions in sales. So here's my easy-to-follow plan for turning an upset customer into a happy and profitable customer.

Step 1: Affirm

Most organizations engage with upset customers by citing policies and procedures. This, of course, is the kiss of death. It's okay to have procedures and policies, but if you start there, you fail. My recommendation is to start by proclaiming to the customer that you intend to listen to them and work hard to make them happy. For example, say, "Ms. Johnson, I understand why you're upset about your room reservation, and I'm very sorry for the inconvenience. Our notes show that you did in fact request a poolside room, and I just want you to know that I intend to make this right."

Step 2:
Listen

One of the hardest things to do sometimes is to simply *shut up*. Our natural instinct is to talk our way through the problem. However, I've found that upset customers need to release steam and talk about why they're upset. So if they want to talk, you need to listen. And if you listen carefully, you discover what you can actually do to make the customers happy.

Step 3:
Confirm

It's not only important that you understand why the customer is upset. You also need to *make the customer know* you understand why they are upset. So, at this point, you need to confirm what you heard the customer say. "Ms. Johnson, I just want to confirm that your preference is a poolside room. You requested a poolside room, and you would like us to offer some compensation for our mistake. Is that correct?"

Step 4:
Fix

The customer has told you exactly why they're upset, you have confirmed why they're upset, and now it's your turn to offer a solution based on what you learned from carefully listening. In the first step you acknowledged that your reservation department made a mistake, and you apologized for the inconvenience. However, the customer still expects you to show your commitment to solving the problem.

At this point you might suggest the following: "Ms. Johnson, I have directed our front desk staff to put you on a priority list should a poolside room come available. In the meantime, can I pay for your buffet breakfast during your stay here as a way of offering our sincerest apologies for the inconvenience?" During the listening phase, you more than likely got hints as to what you should offer to make this particular customer happy. (Unfortunately, too many organizations do not empower team members to "bend the rules" to make a customer happy. From a profitability and customer retention perspective, this is a colossal mistake.)

Step 5:
Follow Up

You may have assumed that you fixed the problem by offering something to the customer in Step 4. However, the customer needs you to revisit the situation with an unexpected follow-up one to two weeks after the incident.

"Ms. Johnson, I just wanted to follow up on the mistake we made with your poolside room reservation a couple of weeks ago. Did the new room and our complimentary breakfast meet with your approval?" This gives you the opportunity to do a quality assurance check to make sure what you offered did in fact leave the customer happy. From the customer's perspective, this demonstrates that making the situation right was truly a priority for you and your organization.

Great organizations love their customers and sincerely want them to be happy. You will see amazing results if you apply this proven formula to your customer conflicts.

TRADER JOE'S:
EXCEPTIONAL TO THE CORE

Trader Joe's (colloquially known as TJ's) is a funky grocery chain that began in 1967 in California, and over the decades expanded throughout the country. It delivers an ideal core experience every time and is a great example of an organization that really understands its customers. The stores are always well staffed and full of money-spending customers, and I can't think of a punitive policy that Trader Joe's has. It is truly a customer-centric organization designing core (and other) exceptional experiences, both digital and non-digital, that are relevant and appeal to several customer types. While all TJ's touchpoints are exceptional, here we'll look primarily at the core experience.

The Product

In order to deliver a great customer experience, you must first deliver a great product or service—duh! Surprisingly, however, many organizations deliver mediocre products and services. Not surprisingly, the customer ends up disappointed.

Most supermarkets sell several different brands of canned corn, for example. Trader Joe's decided, brilliantly, that if you find the very best product, you don't need to offer a dozen options, so TJ's has a minimal selection of canned corn. As In-N-Out Burger taught us, crisp, minimal options reduce confusion and eliminate stress for customers.

Trader Joe's begins the core experience with minimal options, but these minimal options are always exquisite; in fact, they're really exquisite. This reduced number of selections—all quality—allows TJ's to significantly shrink the footprint of its stores. So, not only is the company's cost reduced, but customers can make their shopping experience quick and efficient.

Trader Joe's carries special label products using its own brand name. These are often unique and targeted to a season or holiday. In the fall, you can literally buy all things pumpkin. The produce is exquisitely fresh and well thought out. In fact, the products are so well researched and developed that there are dozens of Trader Joe's cookbooks specifically designed to create affordable, healthy, and delicious meals using store ingredients.

The Price/Value Balance

Trader Joe's does not charge a premium price for its excellent products, nor is it a low-price retailer delivering mediocre products at a cheap price, all the while requiring you to bag your own groceries.

Instead, TJ's believes that exceptional products can be delivered for the same price as mediocre products, and its business model proves the company can do it. Any retailer can provide low-cost but inferior products; Trader Joe's realizes that if it invests time and effort in finding exquisite products, it can also deliver them at a reasonable price.

Although I'm not privy to the finer details of its product costs, I assume that if TJ's sells a larger quantity of one brand of exceptional corn, rather than a smaller quantity of several brands, it can significantly improve its buying power. In turn, it passes on the cost savings to its customers and thereby offers competitive prices and higher quality.

I use the term "customer" loosely when referring to Trader Joe's. I believe that most of its customers would describe themselves as true fans of this amazing business. Great products at an incredibly competitive price make for a great relationship. This formula is critical to the core experience.

The Power of Fun!

As discussed earlier, we humans are multisensory creatures. Each minute we are engaged in an experience, we receive thousands of data points that we aggregate to an opinion of that experience.

Trader Joe's has created a retail environment that can first and foremost be described as being fun! Most organizations are afraid to use the word *fun*. This is unfortunate because people like to have fun. Many consumers describe grocery shopping as drudgery, but that's certainly not the case at Trader Joe's.

TJ's employees sport Hawaiian shirts, and stores are often customized with murals depicting local sites. Products are positioned with great pride; it reminds me of an old-fashioned fruit stand. Free samples of delicious paired ingredients are available every day, and you can always try the latest freshly brewed coffee.

Trader Joe's appeals to several customer types because the stores focus on delivering high-quality food in a great environment. It is a true, exceptional core experience.

To paraphrase world-famous motivational speaker Brian Tracy, "The universe loves a specialist." What Brian means is that when you dedicate yourself to bringing unique value to a customer and market, you win every time. Trader Joe's does not sell the usual supermarket staples like bleach, hardware, or mops. It concentrates on providing exquisitely thought-out delicious and healthy food in a small, convenient retail environment that is fun and engaging. As a result, it has built a fan base across several consumer types.

The Employees Who Deliver to the Core

Trader Joe's treats its employees like royalty, and for this reason it attracts some of the best talent to its fun and diverse environment. You can just see how much the employees enjoy their jobs.

This may sound obvious, but when employees hate their work, they tend to hate their customers. When employees love their work and the company they work for, they deliver far better human experiences.

The Bottom Line

Trader Joe's does not give interviews about its business strategies, but it doesn't take much analysis to see that the core experience TJ's delivers is special. It's pretty obvious this company cares about its employees, its communities, and most certainly the customers it serves.

While this type of core experience is easy to talk about, it's actually quite hard to do. This is why most companies never really commit to being exceptional. I believe that Trader Joe's wants to be good for goodness's sake, and this is the key. The success it's enjoying derives from that commitment. Maybe another business can be successful by replicating what TJ's does solely for the sake of profit, but I've yet to see it happen. TJ's focus is on how it can serve the community the stores reside in. This ranges from sustainability, to how the company treats its employees, to how it communicates with the customers it loves. Everything is centered on a core philosophy of doing good business, which is a centerpiece of the best organizations.

In my local TJ's, management actually has its employees read books on providing exceptional customer service. The managers look at doing the right thing for the customers, rather than squeaking out profits and instituting punitive policies. The best organizations have integrity; they care about those they serve and want to serve them well. As a customer service snob and a patron of Trader Joe's, I can say that the stores have never disappointed me. Because of the work I do, I look at all businesses hyper-critically. I'm always looking for ways to improve on what someone has created, and from my vantage point TJ's is as near perfect as it gets. So, congratulations, Trader Joe's: you are exceptional to the core.

"If you work just for money, you'll never make it,
but if you love what you're doing and you always
put the customer first, success will be yours."
—RAY KROC

HOW TO BUILD YOUR CORE TOUCHPOINT PLAN

If you want to be as good as Trader Joe's, you need to start with the philosophy of goodness. I know it sounds corny, but this is the essence behind the best companies in the world. We live and thrive in a connected economy, and the better we are at creating authentic, mutually beneficial connections, the better our businesses prosper.

Here's how to build the perfect core experience:

Define Your Mission and Understand Why It Is Important. In researching thousands of companies, I found a key determinant of the success of the best organizations in the world: the power of "why."

The mission of the very best, most successful, most profitable companies is centered upon the goal of serving a well-defined customer and market. When I ask people at successful companies why they do what they do, it's all about serving a mission that includes their community, their employees, and of course their customers. When I ask people at failing companies why they do what they do, the answer typically is profit and sales. Isn't that an interesting observation?

Start at the top with a clear and crisp understanding of why you do what you do. If you center your answer on your community, employees, and customers, all of your programs, policies, products, and services will derive from that overarching mission. If yours is a good mission and you are truly committed to it, you get to win.

Make sure your enterprise mission statement is more than a bumper sticker. Make sure your why is community-, employee-, and customer-centric. Make it part of your organization's DNA.

Be Sure You Mean It!

If you say you're committed to delivering exceptional customer experience, but you develop and deliver policies that punish your customer, you'll create a core experience that will fail.

Your customers are smart and they're paying attention. Never design a mission you're not committed to.

Create a mission that matters.

Mean it.

Do it.

Your employees will follow with enthusiasm.

Don't Play Follow the Loser. Many organizations follow the prevailing norm because it eliminates their need to commit to innovation and take on risk. It's simply easier and (seemingly) safer to adopt the commonly accepted and expected business practices. However, with innovation and the corresponding risk comes the opportunity to really excel in your industry or organization.

For example, Trader Joe's has developed a shopping flow using the small store footprint of eight thousand to twelve thousand square feet. (The average is thirty thousand square feet, and some supermarkets are vastly larger.) However, this "risk," given the company's overall strategy, is actually an advantage to customers and a colossal advantage to Trader Joe's. This innovation saves money on rent while significantly improving the shopping experience for the customers. Don't imitate. Innovate! Trader Joe's did and it worked.

Conduct an Innovation Intervention. If you really want to build an exceptional core experience, conduct an "innovation intervention." Bring in customers—and, if possible, critics—and get their take on your core experience.

A friend owns a local restaurant, and for a while had a devastating 3.5 out of 5 Yelp rating. It was killing his business. He called me and asked me to recommend internet reputation companies to help fix the problem. (Companies exist that post good reviews as part of a strategy to push down bad reviews in the overall ranking.)

I suggested that before he attempted to fix his ranking through digital witchcraft, we should assess why people rated him poorly. After a tough discussion, it turned out that, if anything, his ratings were more than fair.

As a result, we reached out to every single person who posted a derogatory rating of the restaurant. We offered to refund the cost of their meal if they would come to a thirty-minute innovation intervention at the restaurant. Many agreed, and a virtual tribe of dissatisfied customers showed up and raked my friend over the coals. It was so bad that this man, who is fifty-five years old, actually cried. In the end, he offered everyone his sincere apology.

I worked with him for a day, and we rebuilt his core experience based primarily on the insights these customers provided. In the end, the customers updated their ratings and posted about how impressed they were that he took the time to hear their grievances. In fact, they became advocates, regularly posting on various rating boards about how great the restaurant was.

In only eight weeks, his rating on both Yelp and TripAdvisor climbed to 4.5 out of 5. His employees enjoyed work more, and my friend learned a valuable lesson: you don't need digital witchcraft.

Fix yourself and you won't have upset customers. As the axiom suggests, "Our business gets better when we get better."

GOOD IS NOT GOOD ENOUGH

Remember, the core experience you provide cannot just meet the baseline level of customer expectation. A good customer experience is about surprising your customer with exceptional products, services, and human experiences. Just because you have to manage operations every single day doesn't mean you can put customer experiences on the back burner.

Develop a philosophy of "customer first, operations second," because I can assure you your best competition does. It's easy to get caught in the minutiae of what writer Dennis Wheatley calls "majoring in minors." There won't be any operations to manage if you don't have customers.

In the connected economy, your customers' expectations climb every day, as does your competition's. So be good to the core!

TAKEAWAYS

The core experience, like all touch moments, is composed of granular micro-moments. The details depend on your individual business, but in a nutshell, it's about how easy it is to do business with you on an ongoing basis. Remember, over time we tend to take our customers for granted, and this can be true of some of our biggest customers. Constantly looking for ways to reinvent the customer experience by removing pain and adding pleasure and convenience drives sales and profit as nothing else can.

Many organizations pay millions of dollars to acquire customer insights, yet they spend virtually nothing on creating and deploying sustainable and outstanding customer experiences. Stand apart and ahead by crafting exceptional core customer experiences, and avoid one of the biggest hazards in business: a risk-centric, internal focus that takes your gaze off your customers' needs and problems. Punitive customer policies serve only you, and your customers respond by drowning you in negative social media ratings.

Think of creating these perfect customer experiences as a design activity. First, develop the skill sets you need to gain actionable insights, and then invent beautiful moments across the entire customer journey. When you are truly outwardly focused on your customers, insights will come at you every single day, and you will then be looking at new innovation plans weekly, not annually.

CHAPTER 10

THE PERFECT LAST TOUCHPOINT MOMENT

Although I am a management consultant, I also speak at dozens of major events around the world each year. In an effort to deliver better talks, I hired a top speaking coach. I know the value of hiring an expert, because that's why people hire me.

The coach was wonderful. To my surprise, what she taught me about delivering a great speech turned out to be one of the most important things organizations can do to deliver a great human experience. What's more, it has everything to do with delivering an exceptional last touchpoint. As she put it, always leave your audience wanting more!

TO GET A STANDING OVATION, ENGAGE YOUR CUSTOMER

You've probably watched amazing TED talks online. These talks are conversational and engaging, and the speakers convey authenticity. In the past, giving speeches meant delivering information to an audience. But today, as my speaking coach explained to me, it's really about connecting to your audience by way of an authentic dialogue. Exceptional communicators aren't talking *at* their audience; they *engage* their audience in an emotional journey even when they are giving a speech. They might ask questions and walk among the audience, or they may do it simply by the way they address them—through the absorbing and relevant content they provide as well as with their mannerisms. Most important, exceptional communicators connect with the audience emotionally; they don't just dump ideas. Poor speakers give talks. Good speakers take their audience on a journey. Good speakers may appear vulnerable and may even look stupid; in other words, good speakers are authentic.

TED talks are strictly limited to eighteen minutes. On the other hand, professional speakers like me are often asked to speak for an hour to an hour and a half, which can feel like an eternity to both the speaker and the listener. Listening to a speaker is much like eating chocolate cake: one piece is delicious, but if you eat the entire cake, you may feel sick.

So the problem my coach and I had to solve was how I could drive the same level of TED engagement over a much longer amount of time and still leave the audience wanting more. The answer: tell them a great story that begins and ends powerfully.

And that's exactly what you need to do to engage your customers. Give them a powerful start and leave them with a memorable ending.

Keep Your Message Running:
Start Strong, End Strong

Often, even professional speakers run out of passion or message be fore they run out of time. This usually results in a weak and squishy ending. Unfortunately, that ending—that last touchpoint—is what the audience remembers forever.

The same is true of your business. It's extremely important that you don't run out of energy or muddy your message toward the end of the customer experience. Most organizations focus on the front end, especially the core experience, but ignore the last-touch—at their peril. Not only is it incredibly important that your customer experience be continuous, consistent, and enticing at all touchpoints, but at the end there's also a huge opportunity to maintain and strengthen your relationship.

Some of my speeches are on the future of the healthcare business. Not long ago, I gave a talk to a global pharmaceutical company. The people who hired me asked me to motivate a large group of executives who were deeply depressed and pessimistic about changes in the industry. Based on what I'd learned from my coach, I knew that to engage this cynical audience, I needed to do something powerful right out of the starting gate, and I had to finish strong.

I began my talk by asking them, "What's your emoji?" As you know, *emoji* is the Japanese word for "picture character." We use this word to represent images such as smiley faces, often in text messages, to convey an emotion.

I had purchased two-dozen smiley face balls, which I threw into the audience at the beginning of my talk. Whoever caught a ball had to tell me their opinion of the future of healthcare. While this made them uncomfortable, it definitely engaged the audience.

As various executives described their often-negative view of the future of healthcare, they were actually setting me up for a talk they would love and remember. After they responded, I provided statistics showing that they weren't alone in their analysis, since most executives in the healthcare industry also believed the future was grim.

Next, I introduced case examples and statistics demonstrating that the industry's future was actually surprisingly good; it was full of potential and offered attractive economic opportunities. I used amusing examples from other industries that had gone through similar changes only to reemerge stronger and more prosperous.

By the end of the presentation and at their final touchpoint, the audience members were excited and saw opportunities they had never before envisioned. I left them laughing and feeling better. I was certain they would remember those smiley face balls and that they had taken away a new way of looking at the future of healthcare. In fact, I heard that, weeks later, some attendees were still talking about the talk. They hadn't just reframed their outlook on the healthcare industry; they had reexamined their worldview, and it affected what they did every day. I made a big impact because I presented the talk in a way that was memorable. And that's what you want to do with the customer experiences you create. You want to touch and engage the customer.

Standing ovation—☺!

WORK IT! KNOW YOUR AUDIENCE

My success as a speaker comes from my willingness to invest an insane amount of time in understanding the unique and special needs—the loves and hates—of my audience. As the smiley face example demonstrates, I also innovate and take risks by presenting ideas in ways my audience hasn't seen or thought of before. No doubt they'd never been bombarded by smiley face balls at any other talks they attended!

That talk was a success because I had gone the extra mile to understand their issues and was able to show them a positive way forward. My vernacular and tone of voice were consistent with my audience's expectations, and at the same time, I delivered on the event organizer's strategy.

Most important, I left my audience wanting more. I didn't run out of energy or powerful content before I ran out of time, and that is the secret of the last touchpoint. Even though your customer has bought into your product, service, or idea, you are not finished. You must continue to provide exceptional service until the very end or your customers will leave with a bad taste and memory. In fact, as you'll see in Chapter 11, their exceptional experience must continue past the point of disengagement.

EMOTIONAL, INTELLIGENT, AND—MOST IMPORTANT—MEMORABLE

Last fall, the worst thing I could imagine happening actually happened. My oldest daughter—whom I love deeply and enjoy living with—left to go to college in San Diego. If you're a parent, then you know how devastating that event can be.

My daughter has always been a joy to be around, and leaving my first baby at school was so much harder than I ever thought it could be. Of course, my wife and I knew that this was what was right for her, but it was still hard. We took her to San Diego and spent some days settling her into her dorm room. I realized this was an important moment for her (as well as for us—in our lives as parents), and I wanted to create a very special last touchpoint. We decided to drive to the beach at sunset to commemorate the occasion. We asked a passerby to take pictures of us looking out into the sunset with our hands raised in celebration (Figure 10-1).

Figure 10-1 My daughter and me in a perfect last-touch moment.

That moment of holding my daughter and raising our arms to the sky as we punctuated an important part of our lives together is unforgettable. I believe we will remember that moment forever. And as business leaders, just as for parents, we need to architect journeys for our customers that are special at each and every touchpoint. Do the last touchpoint well and they will remember it forever.

HOW TO GET THE LAST-TOUCH RIGHT

The next time you buy something, watch for that last touchpoint. Is it being done beautifully? You'll know because you want to come back for more. You feel great about yourself and your purchase. Or did the last touchpoint leave you feeling uncomfortable and with the desire to run away and never come back? If so, there's a lesson there: never do what they did. It's that simple, that personal, and if you do it right, that much fun.

LAST TOUCHPOINTS: LESSONS FROM THE BEST IN THE BUSINESS

The design of your last touchpoint depends on your business, culture, and goals. So, while I can't tell you specifically what to do, I can show you what some extremely successful companies do to manufacture exquisite and relevant last touchpoints.

Burrito Bandito Gets It Right

In practical terms, last touchpoints are digital, non-digital, or in some cases both. Burrito Bandito is a regional California restaurant that delivers great customer experiences across all touchpoints, and the last touchpoint is no different.

When you pay for your burrito and request an email receipt, the people at Burrito Bandito also send an email thanking you for giving them the opportunity to serve you. Included is a simple questionnaire asking for recommendations on how they can serve you better. They have blended the physical last touchpoint (paying for and receiving your burrito) with a digital last touch-point that allows them to continually get better while propagating their desire to authentically serve you.

So, while last touchpoints don't need to be complex or costly, they do need to be relevant, friendly, and authentic.

Nordstrom's Finesse: High Touch, High Quality

Nordstrom, one of the world's leading department stores, provides a great example of delivering meaningful and potent last-touches. The methods used are subtle but powerful. For example, Nordstrom was one of the first companies to have its checkout attendants walk around the counter to personally hand you your shopping bag. Seems like a simple thing, but this gesture has a strong emotional impact.

From a core experience perspective, Nordstrom also provides personal shoppers to take the pain out of finding the perfect suit or dress. The personal shoppers are true professionals; actually, they are more like stylists. For example, they not only know the latest in men's suits, but they also know the right shoes, ties, and pocket squares to go with the suits. They're not pitching to make a sale; they are providing a free consultation service worth hundreds of dollars within the core customer experience.

The exclamation point on the exceptional core experience is the personal last-touch of being handed your shopping bag. If you've experienced this, it's as if your friend handed you your bag before you go. All of Nordstrom's touchpoints lead to shopping in a high-touch, high-quality way.

Starbucks Knows Your Name

When you order your customized drink *du jour* at Starbucks, you are not given a number. Instead, you are quite intentionally asked for your name. Seems like a pretty small thing, but as we have learned, it's the subtleties in human connection that drive amazing human experiences.

The last touchpoint at Starbucks is hearing someone say the most beautiful words in the universe: your name. Studies show that the engagement power of even strangers using your name is incredible, and Starbucks leaves you with this personal connection as an unbelievably powerful last touchpoint.

Starbucks Mangles Your Name

There's more to the Starbucks story. When the baristas started writing customers' names on the cups, it turned out that they often got it wrong. In a noisy coffee shop, it's often difficult to hear clearly, and people spell their names in all sorts of different ways. So a customer named Thomas might see "Tennis" written on his cup, or Rachel might become "Rebel."

In a normal universe, this would be deeply offensive to customers. But this is Starbucks, and the mangling of names has become part of Starbucks mythology. It's become almost like a game.

In fact, many observers believe that misspelling your name is part of a marketing approach that Starbucks has deliberately embraced. Why? Because customers love to go online and post photos of their cups with their bizarro names. The more ridiculous your name appears to be, the funnier it is, and the more hits you'll get.

Is it deliberate? "We have never asked or directed any of our partners to misspell names of our customers for any reason," a Starbucks spokesperson told Thrillist.com. But the fact remains that the improvised names are a hit on social media. #Starbucks-namefail is a popular hashtag on both Twitter and Instagram, and there are Tumblr pages devoted to the topic. There's even a website called "What's My Starbucks Name" that will generate a fanciful version of your name without ever having to set foot into a coffeehouse.

Is it lucky happenstance that Starbucks' mangling of its customers' names is popular with its customers, or is it a deliberate marketing ploy? At this point in time, it's probably a little bit of both.

The Amazing Amazon

Amazon is one of my favorite companies because it knows how to deliver the perfect digital experience. Often when I make a purchase, Amazon suggests other relevant products, some of which are even cheaper.

You could argue that this last touchpoint is an upsell (although, if it is, why are they offering lower-priced items?). But, in fact, Amazon wants the customer to have a memorable digital experience, one that delivers proven value. This is one of the thousands of things that Amazon does extremely well.

Southwest Airlines Leaves Them Laughing

The most appropriate way to describe air travel today is that, even at its best, it's extremely painful. I must travel hundreds of thousands of miles by air each year, and often I fly Southwest Airlines. The company's CEO is famous for saying that Southwest is a customer experience company that happens to fly planes. Quite true.

One of the last touchpoints at Southwest is after the airplane lands and begins to taxi to the jetway. At this point, the captain often comes on the PA system and says something like, "Ladies and gentlemen, we have just landed ten minutes ahead of schedule, and I will have you at the gate shortly. We know you have many options when traveling, and from the captain's chair I would like to offer up my sincerest thanks for choosing Southwest Airlines." More often than not, the announcement is followed by a witty or funny comment from the flight crew that leaves you in a really good mood. They might crack a joke or even sing; one flight attendant actually got the passengers involved when he rapped the entire pre-takeoff message and got them to clap along to the beat.

Tile Man Creates a Customer for Life

I recently hired a contractor to lay tile in my home. He was pleasant and professional and delivered on his promise throughout, but what he did at the end surprised me. When everything was cleaned up and the floor looked fabulous, he asked me if I could sit down for a moment. When I did, this is what he said:

> *"Mr. Webb, I'm a small contractor, and the opportunity to do this kind of work is an honor for me, and I just want to let you know that I appreciate the opportunity to do this work for you. If I can ever be of service to you in any way in the future, it would be a genuine honor."*

He said this with 100 percent sincerity. It wasn't robotic, and he most certainly wasn't faking it. In fact, during his presentation he pulled out his wallet and showed me a picture of his family. We have low expectations for the customer service in this type of work. He wasn't selling a luxury car—he was laying tile. So it really stood out when he showed this exceptional service and touchpoint moment. He made me not just his customer but his advocate. At every opportunity, I recommend him to friends, family, and acquaintances.

What does your last touchpoint look like?

A TOUCHPOINT FROM HELL

I've broken down the touchpoints into manageable bite-size moments so that you can use them as guides to create exceptional experiences. As you have seen, customer experiences are not just a single isolated event but rather a series of events that all have to be perfect. Unfortunately, the last-touch moment is often the most neglected; as a consequence, the result can be terrible.

Five Words That Forever Lost a Customer: "Your Clothes Are Too Heavy"

A few years back, we purchased a new home. Because I do a lot of speaking and meeting with clients, I have more than the usual number of suits, so we asked the builder to add a rotating rack to the bedroom closet to accommodate them. The first night in our home, we were sound asleep when we heard a terrifying crash that came from our bedroom closet. We were shocked to see that the entire rack had collapsed. I contacted the builder the next morning, and the closet subcontractor met me to review the damage. He was extremely talented and friendly and quickly repaired the closet.

When he was done, he called me over to show me the repair so I could sign off on it. So far, so good. But then his last-touch was the kiss of death. "Just so you know," he said, "this wasn't my fault. Your clothes are too heavy." If only he had kept his mouth shut, he might still be in business today. He's not; apparently, I wasn't the only one he mouthed off to.

Thank You for Shopping with Us: How Can I Make You Hate Me?

One of the largest retailers in the country has a well-defined program that encourages cashiers to upsell an extended warranty. Such warranties are extremely profitable for retailers yet rarely deliver value to customers. In fact, if you Google certain retailers' names and add the phrase "extended warranty rip-off," you find thousands of derogatory customer comments verifying that most of the time the warranties are not worth the money.

This short-term gain for long-term pain has become institutionalized in many organizations. Yet treating your customer—who has honored you with their purchase—to a sales pitch to buy something you know does not offer real value is a perfect example of how organizations become extinct. This behavior is not limited to extended warranties. It might be pressuring customers at checkout to sign up for credit cards and other things they simply don't want. To paraphrase the old TV show *Kung Fu*, before you decide to do this, "Choose wisely, Grasshopper."

TAKEAWAYS

Like most touchpoints, the last-touch can be subtle, but it is incredibly powerful as we architect a continuous journey of memorable moments. Think of your last-touch as a way to prove to your customers that you love and cherish the relationship. Surprise them with something terrific, and most important, dig deep and eliminate anything that might be seen as punitive. Last-touch moments are the most ignored touchpoints; yet, as we've seen, they can be the most important.

As you hold brainstorming sessions around the various touchpoint moments, you will become extremely good at finding enjoyable and exciting ways to please your customers. You will also become more granular as you search for the subtle ways that the sounds, smells, visuals, and other impressions can permanently affect the way in which your customers view your product or service. Great organizations like Disney always look for ways to make their experiences across the entire customer journey ten times better than what the customer expected.

This is actually enjoyable work, so lean into it. Cocreate these experiences with your stakeholders so they can feel a sense of ownership. If you do, the financial benefits can be massive, the quality of your work life escalates, and you bulletproof your business from the competition.

CHAPTER 11

THE IN-TOUCHPOINT MOMENT

Whether you provide a product or service, you have an advantage because you know what your customer is interested in. Therefore, you have the opportunity to leverage your content creation and marketing efforts to become a thought leader and value provider, even if the recipient is no longer a customer. This is the spirit of the in-touchpoint.

The concept behind the movement around content marketing is to nurture existing and past customers by sending them a constant stream of value. If you're selling skateboards, for example, then push out the latest or most complex technology. Customers are served by the content, and you're the content expert now. You're the thought leader and value provider.

I once bought a 3D printer from MakerBot. Since then, the company continues to push out valuable information to help me stay on top of changes in the 3D printer industry. The content provided isn't promotional but informational; MakerBot delivers packets of relevant information and therefore value. The company provides exceptional in-touch moments.

The key is to resist the temptation to interrupt customers by trying to sell them more stuff. We need to be more relevant to our customers by delivering thoughtfully designed packets of value to prove we're not trying to sell them anything. In that way, they have a positive feeling about us, and in the future, they will come to us first should they need something we sell.

It's the same concept as in the pre-touch moment: giving value without asking for anything in return. The cycle is complete. In a connected economy, we must be willing to identify areas of value for our customers, and then leverage that value through digital and non-digital channels. At the same time, our approach should be nonintrusive, non-"sales-y," and authentically helpful. Companies that do the in-touch well make their customers' lives better.

THE VALUE PROPOSITION:
RESIST TEMPTATION NOW AND LOOK TO THE FUTURE

Unfortunately, most organizations take a "kiss-on-the-first-date" approach and immediately attempt to leverage the information they have on customers to further sales. Typically, the result is pushback. Customers are not interested in doing business with an organization that leverages their contact information expressly for the purpose of selling more products and services. If this method ever worked, it won't work today. You must stand out by providing value and asking for nothing in return.

For some reason, marketers can't resist the temptation of trying to sell existing customers something new. They view existing customers as low-hanging fruit and market them to death.

But in our hyper-connected economy, the customer is now king (or queen). They need to be courted before they're kissed. Today's customer continually expects free value. If we're smart, we recognize that customers have unlimited options and are going to use them to connect with companies that constantly deliver value. In many cases, that value is absolutely free.

THE POWER OF A VALUE BANK

Many of my clients have adopted a program we call the value bank. The concept is pretty simple: it's the reverse of the usual con game. Con artists always tell you they're going to give you more than they're actually going to provide. In other words, they sell you value you never receive.

The value bank does the opposite: give something of value to the customer for free. My clients even include a post-sale giveaway in our budget. I know of a large asphalt company that develops sports courts. Within its bid is a $700 value bank, and just before its workers are ready to finish a job, they show up with basketball nets and hoops, trash cans, and a treasure trove of cool accessories that their customers didn't expect.

In another example, a Jacuzzi company I know of delivers its Jacuzzis with an enormous basket of spa goodies.

Most organizations just deliver what people expect. What we want to do is deliver experiences so exceptional that we receive 5-star ratings on social networks. Value banking is knowing in advance that you will give your customer something unexpected and exceptional. In this way, you always under-promise and over-deliver. If you follow this simple practice, your customers will remember you and treat you well.

The Rewards of the Unexpected

The value bank concept goes beyond the free prize inside the Cracker Jack box. In that case, the prize inside is expected and therefore part of the customers' baseline expectation. Value banking, on the other hand, shocks customers by giving them something they did not expect.

One of my clients operates high-end lodges and resort hotels that are often rustic as befits their mountain locations. They are expensive to operate, and because of their locations, there is a great deal of seasonal downtime; in fact, the company makes 90 percent of its annual revenue during just six months of the year. Providing exceptional customer experience is vital to their ability to stay in business.

Some time ago, the CEO started having his team members take pictures of the guests throughout their stay (with their permission, of course). A few weeks after guests returned home, they would receive a complimentary and beautifully bound photo album. The cost of each photo album for my client was only $40, and the albums were voluntarily put together by staff members during their downtime. What made it seem even more special was that each album was delivered via FedEx (at a cost to my client of less than $20 each). This simple in-touch moment had an amazing financial impact on my client's business. In fact, as a result of what seemed to be a simple idea, annual re-bookings increased by 78 percent.

The story gets even better. Hundreds of customers posted the pictures from their albums on their social media. By asking new guests how they heard of the property, my client was able to track a 20 percent uptick in new bookings to this practice. Today, in addition to the hard copy photo album, guests are also sent a digital photo album that makes it easier for them to share their photos on influential social networks.

Was my client guaranteed this idea would result in increased business? Was there anything about the gift that looked like a sales promotion? No and no, and that's what makes it a perfect in-touch moment.

CONTENT MARKETING:
THE POWER OF FREE

"Content marketing" is the biggest marketing buzzword on the planet today. Unfortunately, the phrase is an inadequate description of what content marketing really is: providing information at no charge to customers that they would otherwise be willing to pay for, with no strings attached. Notice I said **no** strings attached. Many old-fashioned marketers use content marketing as a way to get customer information so they can hammer them with offers.

Here's another way to describe and understand content marketing: giving free but meaningful content for the sole purpose of providing value to customers and potential customers.

This definition is a bit harder to get onto a bumper sticker, but it's certainly an accurate description of how to use content marketing effectively. The massive popularity of content marketing and its hundreds of thousands of success stories proves that staying in touch with your customer in a way that delivers value at no cost to them is essential to maintaining meaningful customer relationships. This is the importance of being in touch.

HOW TIFFANY & CO. STAYS IN TOUCH

Tiffany & Co. famously manufactures beautifully designed high-quality jewelry. The company loves its customers and is an expert when it comes to delivering exceptional experiences across all customer touchpoints.

Tiffany's last touchpoint, for example, has the professional and engaging sales representative hand-wrapping your purchase in the signature Tiffany blue box and wrapping paper. The box is then handed to you in a beautiful Tiffany blue bag. When you buy something from Tiffany, you purchase something special that instantly becomes a personal treasure or family heirloom.

Tiffany's in-touch moments include providing free product ideas that have meaningful and actionable relevance to the customer. As a result, they induce the clients to make additional purchases in the future. But it doesn't end there. Customers often receive a handwritten thank-you note from the salesperson who sold them the product—*not* from the company through some giant mailroom operation, but from the salesperson themselves. It isn't exactly high-tech and it's not a new invention; it's simply something people stopped doing. It doesn't cost much and yet makes an incredibly powerful impression.

S *tudies prove that when doctors call a patient after a procedure to personally ask how they're doing, it significantly reduces the risk of malpractice lawsuits.[1] By doing this, doctors massively increase the likelihood that their patients will refer new patients and post positive comments on social and public rating sites. Given the acquisition cost of patients for many specialties and the disastrous impact a malpractice lawsuit can have, it seems to me that calling a patient after a procedure should be mandatory. Yet, despite the obvious benefits, many doctors simply ignore this step.*

Just in Case:
What a Gentle Reminder Can Do

I have a friend who told me how he and his wife had been transitioning through a rough patch in their twenty-year marriage. Years ago, he had purchased a bracelet for her at Tiffany. Now, a few days before Valentine's Day, Tiffany sent him a gentle reminder (not thirty reminders, just one) that Valentine's Day was coming. He'd totally forgotten.

The reminder contained a handful of thoughtful recommendations. He selected one, went online and made his purchase, and the gift arrived in just two days. Needless to say, his wife was delighted.

This meaningful moment was brought to the couple by Tiffany. Yes, Tiffany wants to sell more products, but the company is extremely thoughtful and judicious in the way it delivers information that matters to its customers.

IN-TOUCH MOMENTS:
PERSONAL, RELEVANT, AND VALUABLE

The bottom line for most consumers is that they don't want companies contacting them unless they come bearing gifts. The best organizations stay in touch with their customers by offering real, valuable benefits that are not designed for the specific purpose of selling more products and services.

It's okay to make money as a result of staying in touch with your customer, but if your principal goal is to make money, you're going to fail miserably. Your in-touch offers should be exclusive and meaningful. For this reason, you must carefully manage the frequency of these offers. The purpose of staying in touch with customers is to maintain personal, relevant, and valuable contact.

My kids have braces and our dentist sends them texts to remind them to brush their teeth or tell them which foods to avoid and so on in the name of healthy teeth and undamaged braces. It's a way to stay in touch frequently and isn't an attempt to sell us anything. The dentist is just helping my kids have a better experience. In this way, the dentist is using connectivity to add value.

I n addition to making in-touch offers and communications personal, relevance is extremely important. Office Depot knows that I own an HP printer. The company also knows the model. Using its customer relationship management tools for good instead of evil, Office Depot can make me surgically precise offers for inkjet and laser cartridges it knows I need and ultimately want.

The best use of CRM tools is for providing information and opportunities that are exceedingly germane to your customer types. Respect me by not pushing out a bunch of stuff I don't need. Instead, send me offers applicable to me, and you will have a customer for life.

HOW TO DESIGN THE RIGHT IN-TOUCH MOMENTS

Personal, relevant, and *valuable* are the three essential design characteristics of exceptional and lasting in-touch experiences across all your customer types. They are what is important to your customers, and if you meet those needs, you create not just outstanding in-touch moments but, more important, lifelong clients.

No matter the size of your company, exquisite in-touch moments are within your reach. This is where CRM software comes into play for smaller companies that might not have the resources of Office Depot or Tiffany. Inexpensive CRM applications can search by the kinds of products and services individuals have purchased. This information allows you to push out pertinent information that will be of value to that customer type.

Here are some ways to design perfect in-touch moments for your customers.

Make It Personal

It's important to identify ways to *customize* your communication with customers at all connection points so as to engage them in ways that mechanized approaches simply don't. As I have said throughout this book, exceptional customer experiences are about inventing connections that deliver meaningful and real value.

Creating and perpetuating these personal connections requires innovation; in some cases, it requires a new business model. The good news is that individualizing your communications to your customers will make you a hero. You will build relationships far more significant than the sterile ones most companies have.

The Personal Checklist

Ask yourself:

❏ Have you taken the time to know your customers well?

❏ Do you know their customer types?

❏ Do you communicate with the express purpose of providing customers with free and meaningful value?

❏ Do you provide them with incredibly relevant offers they immediately recognize as valuable?

❏ Do you choose carefully when and how you stay in touch?

❏ Do you resist the knee-jerk reaction to reach out to your customers just to sell them products and services?

Make It Relevant

Many organizations cast a wide net when they push out offers to their customers in the hope that they can sell them something.

Their mistake is that they're not making the offers relevant to the customers. You certainly aren't relevant if you send a special offer on women's shoes to men who want suits. Yet this kind of irrelevant output happens all the time as companies desperately and irresponsibly push out broad-based offers. Don't fall into this trap.

Once you understand your customers through their customer types and purchasing habits, you can tailor your offers to what's *relevant* to them—just as Office Depot does to sell me HP printer cartridges.

The Relevant Checklist

Ask yourself:

- ❏ Do you provide offers based on a past purchase that makes them relevant to this customer?

- ❏ Have technologies, styles, or other elements changed the environment that would make the offer irrelevant?

- ❏ Have you identified the customer type so well that you can make this customer an extremely granular offer?

- ❏ Have you done enough heavy lifting to know the categories of goods and services this customer might actually like to know about?

- ❏ Is the offer overly general (for example, announcing a sale)? Or are you providing a special offer that's unique and targeted to that customer?

❏ Will your customer acknowledge this offer as having relevant meaning and benefit?

Make It Valuable

If you're like me, your inbox is full of offers that have absolutely no value to you whatsoever. In fact, the offers have so little value that it's an insult they were even sent to you. All they do is demonstrate how little the sender cares about you or understands what's relevant to you. Examine your offers closely to see if you're really delivering value or if you're just looking after your bottom line.

The Value Checklist

Ask yourself:

❏ Does the offer look like you're trying to sell the recipient something, or does it look like you're providing the customer with something they really care about?

❏ Do you push out offers to customers more than once a month?

❏ Have you circulated the offer with your customer advisory group or other customer-facing stakeholders to see if you are really offering value?

❏ Have you developed a method to measure how frequently your customers want to be contacted and the kind of value they're looking for?

THE IN-TOUCH BIG PICTURE

Your customers will stay engaged if you deliver great products and services via beautiful experiences across all customer touchpoints and throughout digital and non-digital channels.

Unfortunately, almost all in-touch experiences from companies have nothing to do with customer experience and everything to do with cross-selling or upselling a customer a new product or service. Having your customer's contact information is a privilege. You should handle this honor with great respect. You should use it in a way that constantly delivers more engagement and value to your customer.

The best companies are in touch with you in a gentle and appropriate way, and your life gets better as a result of their being in touch with you. This is what the in-touchpoint is all about.

TAKEAWAYS

In the exciting sandbox I get to play in, I have the honor of watching great companies invent incredibly clever in-touch moments, from cardiology practices that provide free heart monitoring applications, to swimming pool companies that deliver a New Year's "Splash Kit" to help customers get their pool swim-ready for spring.

You can simply copy other people's ideas when necessary, but if you want to be a superstar, invent your own incredible ways to deliver ongoing and meaningful value to current and past customers. Don't worry that you are wasting money on customers who may never come back. Worry about becoming irrelevant to your customers by not continuing to work the relationship.

I know many people from high school who continue to be my friends today. The only reason we're still friends is that we decided to continually reach out to one another and add value to our respective relationships. So is the case with your customers. It's a conscious choice to make yourself amazing at each and every one of the five touch moments. Most organizations never do this, and they take a financial hit from organizations willing to do the heavy lifting of understanding their customers' loves and hates and transmuting those insights into perfect human moments across each and every touchpoint.

CHAPTER 12

TECHNOLOGY AND THE FUTURE
OF CUSTOMER EXPERIENCE

Technology as it relates to customer experience can be a double-edged sword. On one side, many organizations lean on old-fashioned technology, such as Net Promoter Score methods, customer relationship management tools, and digital surveys. Virtually all of these provide erroneous and fractional insights about what customers truly love and truly hate. Yet installing some form of technology often gives many executives a warm, comfortable feeling. It's as if doing so removes the responsibility of really getting to know and understand their customers.

On the other side of the blade is the fact that there's no doubt that good technology can provide better insights and ways of aggregating and responding to those insights. But if this is done poorly, it usually results in failure.

Therefore, I recommend that organizations develop an integrated power plan that includes both digital and non-digital channels. It should also include technology stacks, which are ranges of technologies that help you do a better job of identifying what customers need and want and how to deliver better solutions to them. In this way we use the powerful insight-gaining potential of technology for the right purpose—to deeply understand what our customers love and what they hate.

Without a complete and integrated plan, chances are we will just lean on old-fashioned, fractional approaches toward customer experience. We will assume that customer relationship programs—typically marketing programs—are going to save the day. Of course, as we've seen throughout this book, they can't.

TECHNOLOGY AS POWER

Earlier, I suggested that you have to stay away from focusing on technology. In this chapter, however, I'm saying you should use technology. Do I contradict myself? Not really.

What I'm suggesting is that the old-fashioned methods—often CRM programs—of leveraging technology were really about trying to find new ways to push out sales pitches to customers. The problem with that is customers don't want to be managed. They want to be honored and respected.

So, as we begin the process of leveraging technology, we do it from the perspective that the technology we use will enable a more efficient and effective job of delivering surprising value to the customer across both digital and non-digital channels. If we start from that perspective, the insights gathered will be far more relevant and will move us toward innovation and customer experience superstardom.

FIVE KEY DRIVERS OF TECHNOLOGY FOR THE LONG TERM

Here are the five key drivers that will determine the success of your enterprise as it relates to technology. Regardless of changes in the foreseeable future, these drivers will remain relevant, and they will be applicable to the way you build your customer experience power plan. They will affect the use and benefit of technologies over the next several decades.

Driver #1:
Digital Ubiquity

One of the most conspicuous trends that will change the way in which customers engage us, the way we engage them, the way we gain insights, and the way we measure and monitor the results of the products and services we deliver to the market is the concept of digital ubiquity. This is the idea that digital connectivity is everywhere, and it will only become more so.

The way in which we leverage the advantage of being continuously connected to our customers will have a massive impact on the way we deliver and build delicious customer experiences. Digital ubiquity says our customers can find us, research us, vet us, and try to glean value from us. They're engaging our products, services, and brand through connected devices.

Today, those connected devices are likely mobile devices. As I mentioned in Chapter 1 and explained with the Google example, micro-digital moments (or micro-moments) are incredibly important in terms of how a customer engages and connects to a brand. Tomorrow, this digital ubiquity will only expand as our connected devices come in the form of wearable technologies.

There is digital ubiquity today in that we're all connected. In the next wave, we will of course still always be connected, but we will be connected to a great many more things and in more ways than we are now. We will be in touch with our customers, they will be in touch with us, and we will have the advantage of the ability to glean data and insights as never before.

So how is your organization going to leverage the fact that your customer today is digitally ubiquitous—and will be even more so in the future—and constantly connected? What are you going to do to leverage your connection to your customer and create amazing experiences? We must create seamless, integrated, and elegant connections blending both digital and non-digital human experiences.

One problem I find many organizations have is that they create two customer experience silos: (1) the real world, non-digital, side, where team members build real-life experiences for their customers, and (2) the digital side, where the team builds out digital experiences. Regrettably, organizations often do a poor job of seamlessly integrating the two.

The trick is to always build out these experiences concurrently with your entire team to ensure that the products, services, delivery channels, and branding square up to create one integrated solution. In this way, your digital ubiquity and your digital brand promise will be in sync with the non-digital physical, real experiences you also provide.

Driver #2:
Granularity

In the past, our tools for obtaining consumer data were poor. Often, the information was so vague that we were unable to use it to come up with customer-driven innovations. Fortunately, today we are able to be extremely granular. We don't just look at pet owners, for example; we can look at female owners of French Bulldogs who live in Brooklyn.

The more granular we become, the better we will be at delivering relevant messaging, and the better job we will do of delivering products, technologies, and services that the customers we serve consider excellent. Technologies will continue to afford us the ability to have far greater granularity in the way in which we identify our customer types, and because of this, we will be able to build packets of solutions that are very, very relevant to them.

Remember, historically we were designers of macro-customer experiences. Today, we must be micro-designers, designing micro-experiences to micro-segments of a subsegment. It may seem ridiculous to get that granular, but through technology we have the ability to do it, and because we have the ability to do it, we should do it.

The headwater of excellent customer experience is really relevance. If we want to create relevant experiences, we must become more granular in understanding the unique segments and subsegments of all our customer types so we can build out messaging and solutions that are special to them.

Driver #3:
Meaningful Data

The third trend is meaningful data. Cognitive computing, a subset of artificial intelligence that is typically used to describe AI systems designed to simulate human thought, is one of the most exciting areas in big data and data analytics. Not only must we get lots and lots of data (because, well, we can), but we also need to understand what that data means. Every data signal has meaning. We need to look at every piece of data and leverage the power of cognitive computing to understand ways to deliver better experiences. Many times this will happen in ways we never thought of.

The future of technology, as it relates to customer experience and to meaningful data, will have much to do with acquiring large amounts of data sets. Cognitive computing will take that data and do a far better job of aggregating and leveraging it to understand its full meaning. Once we begin to see these small signals, we can identify unique and special ways to deliver perfect human experiences.

Several great organizations are already in this business. Certainly, for example, IBM Watson is full speed ahead developing a wide range of technologies and solutions for understanding the meaningfulness of data. For these reasons, cognitive computing will be the next big technological wave in customer experience design.

Social listening is another exciting area in big data and data analytics. Analyzing the voice of the customer through social media data provides organizations with the ability to understand consumers as they never have before. Consumers share hundreds of billions of posts about their experiences, likes, and dislikes every year.

Customer experience and marketing executives can not only use social data to measure brand health and the impact of marketing campaigns on purchase intent, but they can also use this data to identify unmet needs in the market to inform future product innovation.

Using cutting-edge big data analytics techniques, you can perform virtual ethnography at scale. Organizations that tap into unsolicited social data have a distinct advantage over those that rely only on traditional, solicited data (such as surveys) that frequently merely confirm what they already know, thereby perpetuating the status quo.

Driver #4:
Actionable Insights

Actionable insights derive from having meaningful data; this means having information we can actually do something with. *Duh!* Seems pretty obvious, but I have witnessed millions, and in some cases tens of millions, of dollars spent obtaining insights that were all one-dimensional and meant virtually nothing. In the future, the beauty of technology—the elegance and poetry of technology as it relates to customer experience—will be our ability to understand the meaning of what our customers are doing, what they're saying, and how they're behaving.

When we are able to understand the meaning of our customers' behaviors, we have the nucleus of what we need to create disruptive innovations that will blindside our competition while delighting our valued customers.

Driver #5:
Measurability

The last trend in the future of technology is measurability. As we in the management consulting field say, "What gets measured gets done."

Sadly, too many organizations are involved in initiatives that either can't be measured or use incorrect measurement tools. Therefore, most organizations have little ability to determine the success of a range of initiatives. Worse, some organizations measure only the success of an initiative based on its profitability, without regard to its impact on the customer and the market the organization serves.

Measurements should be in the form of executive dashboards, which allow you to take lots of complex data (that might normally appear in a spreadsheet) and deliver it to the user in a simple graphic way. Anything you can measure can go into this simple graphic interface. An executive dashboard is a handy tool that allows you to clearly see the effect of current customer experience initiatives and to pinpoint ways to improve your customers' experiences based on the data. Setting up a wide range of powerful measurement tools and reporting them to key executives via executive dashboards is by far one of the most powerful technologies that will serve the future of customer experience, particularly as the data and methods by which it is delivered will continue to improve in the future.

Most organizations look at the way they impact customers annually or—surprisingly—they never do it. However, by using executive dashboards that are in the hands of people who have the authority, the inclination, and the motivation to make changes quickly, you can make sure your company doesn't go off track. Your organization can be proactive instead of reactive. In our hyper-competitive environment, by the time we realize we're headed down the wrong road, it's often too late. We've been blindsided by the competition because we didn't have the pulse of our market, our customers, and their entire journey at our fingertips.

Executive dashboards leveraging cognitive computing and better insights across the customer experience are the future of customer experience.

A word of warning: don't use technology as a way to drive profit. Technology can increase efficiency, reduce costs, and build sales. But if this is your principal focus, chances are you'll be delivering mediocre customer experiences. You can't develop an awesome customer experience or an organizational culture that is customer-centric just by using technology! Don't fall into the lazy person's trap of plugging in a technology stack and waiting for your happy customers to give you a 5-star online rating. It won't work.

TAKEAWAYS

These five trends will morph in many different ways. Some of them are in development stages and some are already available.

Digital ubiquity is here and will continue to be more so as new sensors and technologies are invented.

Granularity is the only way we can create real and meaningful experiences across a wide range of customer experiences.

Meaningful data, understandable information about what our customers really care about, is essential. The key to managing lots of data is the ability to aggregate it and identify what matters.

The ability to come up with meaningful data through cognitive computing and social listening will have a major impact on the way we identify meaning. It will allow us to have **actionable**

insights to transform what we learn into innovations that deliver exceptional customer experiences instantaneously over long developmental life cycles.

And finally, **measurability** via graphic user interfaces or executive dashboard interfaces will allow us to get complicated information reported to a range of executives quickly so that they have the authority, motivation, and inclination to move fast and improve the quality of our customer experiences.

These five technology drivers should be part of everything you do as you build your power plan. There is no doubt technology will have an incredible impact on the future of the customer experience.

CHAPTER 13

YOUR ROADMAP TO
WHAT CUSTOMERS CRAVE

As the adage states, "Failing to plan is planning to fail." This is certainly the case when you design customer experiences to grow your business and protect you from the competition. The bad news is one size does not fit all. Your roadmap needs to fit the unique and special needs of your business, your customers, and the market you serve.

With this in mind, I have created an action plan that allows you to ask the right questions so you can design the right experiences for your business. As you build your plan, remember that this is a dynamic process. You can't create a plan once a year and assume it will remain forever relevant in our fast-changing economy. Rather, your plan is an ongoing process of gaining better customer insights, leveraging enabling technologies, and continually addressing societal and market changes. Some of my clients live in such dynamic spaces that they review their roadmap weekly. View your roadmap to what your customers crave as a continual, enjoyable, and ever improving process.

WHY CUSTOMER INITIATIVES FAIL

In one sense, airplanes are potentially explosive metal tubes flying through the air. Based on this fact, you might assume that statistically they would be incredibly unsafe. However, statistics show instead that, based on miles traveled, traveling by air is safer than traveling by automobile.

How is it that airplanes are so unbelievably safe? The answer is simple: the preflight checklist. This one tool ensures that the pilot and copilot have checked all the operational and safety systems in the plane prior to takeoff. Most of these systems also have redundancy designed into them to significantly reduce the risk of catastrophic failure.

Statistically, the overwhelming majority of customer experience initiatives fail. The primary reason for this isn't that those in charge didn't perform the preflight checklist. No, the biggest cause of failure is that they never created the checklist in the first place.

THE PRE-CUSTOMER EXPERIENCE INITIATIVE

In the spirit of the preflight checklist, we need to begin this somewhat linear roadmap by first setting up a solid foundation. These steps help you determine if you have the enterprise culture to act upon your roadmap.

Develop a Strategic Plan

As a management consultant, I'm absolutely shocked at how many organizations are attempting to achieve organizational growth and market mastery when they don't even have a strategic plan. I recently worked with a $6 billion company that was more than one hundred years old and its last strategic plan was created in the 1960s. Not surprisingly, this company was failing and desperately needed help.

In order to succeed at delivering an exceptional customer experience, you need to travel upstream to the headwaters of strategic success. This requires that you build out a powerful, actionable, and sustainable strategic plan that includes the following key components:

1. Mission Statement: The most successful organizations in the world have a well-defined reason to exist. Conversely, organizations with a vague or ill-conceived concept typically fail. I've had the honor of working with some great brands, and I have found that the best ones are mission-centered. In addition, the leaders of these organizations do an extremely good job of articulating their vision.

Therefore, a good strategic plan should begin with a mission statement. Personally, I like a mission statement that is short, sweet, and easy to brand to both the market and stakeholders. It should be uncomplicated and without industry jargon; it should also state how your business serves people.

In Chapter 4, I presented some examples of mission statements of great organizations like Google, Amazon, and Apple. These statements are all about a big mission to do good for others. This is particularly important as you try to attract and keep millennial talent. Millennials are not looking for a job. They're looking to be part of an important movement.

2. Strategic Goals and Pillars: Downstream from your organization's mission statement lie your goals, which directly serve your mission. In turn, these goals are extremely important because they are the target that your strategies are aiming for.

The extraordinarily talented executive team of the hospital chain for which I consult renamed their goals "strategic pillars." What I like about this approach is that the strategic pillars don't change every week; rather, they are hardwired into the culture of the business. The pillars essentially hold up the organization by giving everyone a clear, crisp vision of why stakeholders come to work every day.

Strategic, well-defined pillars also provide a wonderful way to articulate strategic initiatives by connecting the two together. I suggest you come up with no more than six and no fewer than four pillars or goals.

3. Strategic Initiatives: This is where the rubber meets the road. These initiatives are detailed tactics you use to serve your strategic pillars or goals. One of the biggest problems with strategic initiatives is getting them adopted by your stakeholders.

I was recently engaged by a multibillion-dollar company to help it build out a more intelligent enterprise strategy. I interviewed more than forty-five executives, and every single one told me the reason their strategies had bad returns was that every week there was a new strategic initiative.

One executive actually became angry as she told me that she couldn't take it anymore. She explained that every week there was a new strategy, and before she had time to serve that strategy, another three-ring binder filled with even newer strategies was dropped on her desk. As a result, some employees began ignoring the initiatives because they were overwhelming and a new priority would soon show up anyway.

If you want a winning strategy, make your strategic initiatives count. Connect your initiatives to internal collaborative networks and build engaging games and social connections around your strategic goals. Successful organizations do not shove strategies down to the subordinates. Instead, market-winning organizations collaborate with their stakeholders and work with them to build out the initiatives. Once they have cocreated with the stakeholders who will deploy the initiative, they use social interaction, brainstorming, and game mechanics to significantly increase the returns on the strategy.

4. Measurements: Although last on our list, this is certainly not least. As I've stated, I am a big fan of presenting information and measurements using executive dashboards. These tools help executives get real-time continual information on how a strategic initiative is performing. They provide the feedback necessary to allow stakeholders to understand how their behaviors and activities are affecting strategic results. The best organizations use entertaining graphic interfaces that look like dashboards on video games. When using an executive dashboard, be sure to measure the right stuff: results, not activity.

A Few Caveats on Developing Your Plan

When developing your strategic plan, make sure it is designed so that you don't punish failure, as it is the fuel of innovation. Most organizations have become far too risk averse. They don't encourage courage because they don't want anything bad to happen. Too many organizations don't do great things because they have an obsessive focus on risk. But to succeed, we need to invent new experiences. Thomas Edison failed one thousand times before he successfully invented the light bulb. A progression of failures fueled his success. To go beyond the mediocre, it is often necessary to invent something new; risk is inherent in that. We need to see our mistakes as ways to figure out what to do right. It is essential that you truly collaborate with your team and empower them to innovate and create new ideas for improving strategic performance.

In addition, regrettably, most organizations begin the process of creating a comprehensive customer experience strategy in a silo or vacuum. In other words, the plan is completely disconnected from the overall mission, pillars, and strategic initiatives of the enterprise. As a result, these organizations are incredibly inefficient and often completely off target when building their customer experience strategy. It's extremely important that you finalize your enterprise strategy before attempting to build a world-class customer experience roadmap.

The top 10 killers of enterprise strategy success are:

1. *A weak leader.*

2. *A weak mission statement.*

3. *Lack of collaboration with stakeholders.*

4. *A risk-centered enterprise.*

5. *No digital means of collaboration, engagement, and game playing.*

6. *No way for stakeholders to win in the game of strategy.*

7. *A bad strategic vision centering on profit and revenue rather than on serving others.*

8. *Lack of commitment by leadership.*

9. *Fearful stakeholders who are punished for trying to do the right thing.*

10. *No internal brand plan for strategic success.*

Develop Organizational Life Support Systems

You also need to build your organizational life support systems, including technology stacks, team members, research, tools, processes, systems, and methods. Figure 13-1 is an overview of the five steps that are essential to the creation of any organization's successful strategic plan. It is based on what my company typically creates for our clients.

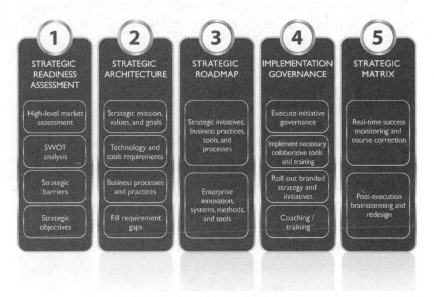

Figure 13-1. Strategy as a managed service.

HOW TO CREATE A PLAN TO
GIVE CUSTOMERS WHAT THEY CRAVE

Now that you've built your strategy, let's create a plan to get you to your goal of becoming the leading provider of world-class customer experiences in your market.

Step 1:
Do the Research

Literally thousands of tools—including social analytics and data sets—are available to help you leverage insights. However, we're concerned here with relevant data that will help you better understand your customer types. Before you begin the process of identifying your ultimate plan to move forward, you need as much relevant data as possible to come up with the best possible plan.

In Chapter 2, we examined the hypothetical NeoWash car wash, where the owner actively observed the way customers engaged the car wash's products and services. The owner conducted regular brainstorming sessions with his team for the express purpose of identifying customer types. They were quickly able to break their customers down into four easy-to-understand customer types, which in turn led to far better insights into what their customers hated and what they loved.

Active observation followed by innovation sessions helped them create the perfect car wash experience for all their customer types. This process also helped them create their journey map as they began to understand what mattered across the range of customer types at each touchpoint.

The more data you can glean prior to building your customer experience roadmap, the more successful you will be.

Step 2:
Collaborate to Innovate

As the saying goes, "Knowing ain't doing." Just knowing what your customer wants, hates, and loves isn't enough. You need to take these insights and turn them into world-class experience innovations.

In the innovation world, we do this quite successfully through collaboration, especially with customer-facing stakeholders and other team members who have the inclination and authority to get the innovations moving.

To facilitate the process of collaboration, it's helpful during brainstorming sessions to use what I call innovation prompting statements and questions. Here are some examples:

- Our customers hate to wait. How can we speed up our service?

- Our customers love value. How do we deliver conspicuous value?

- Our customers are constantly connected. What do our micro-mobile moments look like when people search for our product or service?

- Our service may not meet every customer's expectations. What's our action plan for turning upset customers into customers for life? Should we have a customer advocate with special training who can intervene when things go awry?

- People are multisensory. Have we looked at the smell, taste, sound, feel, and overall emotional experience of our business?

- Innovation occurs in other enterprises. How can we cross-pollinate great ideas from other industries to serve our customers?

- We sometimes do stupid things. What's the dumbest thing we do and how can we stop doing it?

- Customers complain about different things. What's our customers' main complaint, and how can we eliminate it?

- We do a number of things well. What's the best thing about our business, and how can we make it better many times over?

- We know this and this and this about our customers. What do we need to know about them that we don't currently know?

- We are updating our analytic systems. How can we use them to get better real-time insights about our customers' journey?

- We've got lots of information but it doesn't reach all of us until our monthly meeting. How can we push out real-time dashboard data to our stakeholders so everyone can see the impact each of us is having on the overall customer experience?

- We created a new mission statement. Does our entire team understand it? How can we communicate it more effectively?

- We have successfully branded our business in our advertising. Have we internally branded the importance of a customer-centered business to our team?

I could list hundreds of these extremely powerful prompts. However, those presented here will help you quickly answer the most critical questions for mastering the customer experience in your industry.

CONSTRUCTING A CUSTOMER EXPERIENCE IS NOT A ONETIME EVENT

One of the core messages of *What Customers Crave* is that creating exceptional customer experiences for all customer types, across all five touchpoints, via both digital and non-digital means, is not a onetime event. You must constantly live your customers' experiences and then use collaboration and innovative design to make them better and better.

I travel all around the world visiting companies in just about every industry category imaginable. Interestingly, I can put each of these companies into one of two buckets: (1) organizations that want to check the customer experience box and then move on to the next strategy, and (2) organizations where customer experience is truly part of their DNA. For these latter companies, creating customer experiences isn't just an annual event. They talk about these experiences, learn from them, measure them, and live them every single day of the year.

I recently hired a fitness trainer who explained, "Getting fit and healthy is easy in theory. The problem is, it's hard in practice. I can give you the easy stuff—the science—but if you don't do the heavy lifting, you're wasting both of our time. The bottom line is, eat less and work out a lot more. Not exactly new, but it works."

Creating a great customer experience is easy—in theory. The only problem is that it's sometimes hard to pull off in practice. You must understand your customer types and invent amazing experiences for each of them across the five digital and non-digital touchpoints. That requires a sustained focus, the right team, a commitment from leadership, and measurements that allow you to prove return on investment.

NINE THINGS YOU NEED TO DO TO BUILD A GREAT ROADMAP

Below is a nine-point list of the things you need to build your roadmap. These are really all you need. When you have created each of the things listed here and continually connect them to your customers and stakeholders, you will lead your market in exceptional customer experiences.

1. Construct Team Architecture: Before you begin, create a team of customer-facing stakeholders and executive enablers who will give you the insight and authority you need to build the perfect roadmap.

2. Hold Five Fast Brainstorming Sessions: I have found that in only five sessions, you can gain the insights you need to take your amorphous data and turn it into an actionable customer experience roadmap. Schedule either weekly or biweekly sessions with your team. Your goal is to identify your customer types, understand their digital channels, and map their digital and non-digital touchpoints.

3. Begin Innovation Safaris: You must support these sessions with innovation safaris, which will take you and your team on an expedition into the real world of your customers' experiences. There are two types of innovation safaris. One is digital and leverages social analytics to gain insights into what customers are saying about you, your products, and your brand. The other is non-digital. Here, you spend time watching your customers experience your product or service. These real-world insights are extremely powerful and provide practical data about how to create world-class innovations.

4. Cross-Pollinate Ideas: Innovation comes in many forms. Some simply involve repurposing ideas from other companies and markets. There is no shame in borrowing engagement strategies that are working elsewhere. However, plan on making them much better by customizing them to meet the unique needs of your enterprise.

5. Intelligently Implement Technology: Technology for technology's sake is a joke, yet it is widely done. Once you've identified how your customers want to engage you and how you can measure and manage customer data, then and only then should you begin to select technology stacks. As I have warned several times, bad customer service cannot be improved through the use of technology. Technology is nothing more than a servant of a good strategy. Remember, "Choose wisely, Grasshopper."

6. Talk to Your Customers—the Lovers and the Haters: Identify key customers. This includes those who love you so you can get an understanding of what they love so much. It also means those who hate you. Do the same with them so you know why they hate you. Meet with them in person. These gatherings give you real-world insights into how people feel about your business. (One of the hallmarks I want you to take away from this book is that the better we understand our customers, the more able we are to provide them with exceptional and relevant customer service. You'll lose a few nights' sleep over this, but if you're willing to step up and act on these insights, you will positively impact your business and brand.)

Recently, restaurants have started to invite Yelp "haters" to dinner meetings to find out why they rated them so poorly. The benefits can be enormous, as you saw in Chapter 9. First, you learn why these customers hate you, and presumably, you will be able to change or stop doing whatever that is. Second, when haters see that you genuinely want their insights, they may begin to realize that you're doing the best you can to improve your business. Then they'll give it another chance, and more often than not, they will retract their negative ratings and share with the world the powerful and adult way you managed their grievances.

S ometimes haters are your best secret weapon. A few years back, I wrote a book designed to help children learn how to become more innovative. I was shocked when I saw a four-paragraph slam of the book on Amazon. I didn't write the book to make money; I was trying to do something cool. How dare this person insult my innovation prowess?

When I calmed down, I realized that most of what the reviewer said was right. I hadn't put the work into the book that I should have. As a writer, you are the product, and these kinds of reviews are like a baseball bat to the head.

I removed the book from Amazon and decided I would never do something that slapdash again. The hater made me better.

Cautionary note: some haters just hate, and that's it. But even if you assume their grievances are not justified, read their reviews and determine as objectively as you can if there's something there you can learn from. Although you may not always like what's being said, you must set up social monitoring so you always know what is being said about your company, product, service, and brand.

7. Make It Easy and Fun to Understand: As a corporate strategist, I have watched the strategic process of rolling out roadmaps for decades. Somewhere along the way, it became essential that companies have a formal process that everyone is supposed to follow. Hogwash! It's true that how you lay out your roadmap makes a difference, so make it visual—for example, use icons— since that is the best way to communicate ideas and steps. Historically, roadmaps have looked like business plans—dry, boring, and hard to understand. Instead, build your roadmap graphically, make it fun, and make it colorful.

Your roadmap format should be as simple as possible, making maximum use of icons and graphics. If you want to make your roadmap matter, you need to communicate your goals from the janitor all the way up to the executive suite. Everyone needs to understand your mission, goals, strategic pillars, strategies, and measurements. That way, they will be able to participate fully.

Recently, I've noticed that organizations are creating infographics that act as strategic snapshots for their roadmaps. They are easy to understand and are actually fun to look at. In my business, we build roadmaps as graphically thoughtful PowerPoint decks that usually include ten to fifteen slides. It's not a bunch of corporate-speak; it's language everybody can relate to. The format reflects what we stand for, and this is how we are going to achieve it.

The best organizations are careful to bring in baby boomers, GenXers, and millennials to make sure their plan's language resonates across generations. In creating your roadmap, there are a few things that it's important you *don't* do:

- Don't use corporate-speak when creating your plan.

- Don't make it about profit and sales. Make it about an engaging mission.

- Don't build a plan that doesn't have an internal branding strategy.

- Don't have unreasonable expectations of team members.

- Don't mandate results without giving authority to those who must create them.

- Don't be the boss. Be the community leader.

- Don't start a customer experience initiative without your life support system in place.

- Don't start a customer experience initiative without leadership commitment.

- Don't be afraid to play well with others in the enterprise sandbox.

- Don't forget to have *fun*.

8. Don't Go It Alone: Recently, when our dishwasher broke, I decided to fix it myself and save the $150. Turns out I don't know how to fix dishwashers, and the result was a $750 bill. What did I learn? I don't know everything! And there's a chance you don't know everything either, which is why it's extremely important to fill in your competency and skill gaps. I've seen so many failed initiatives that were put together with duct tape and bailing wire. Bring in a great consultant or other adviser to help you get this right. The added benefit is that it will be less stressful and more fun.

9. Measure, Measure, and Then Measure Some More: A well-done customer experience initiative always delivers an impressive return on investment. But before you embark on it, protect the project by proving to other leaders the need for continued funding.

Often, excellent customer experience initiatives are killed because they look like an expense item on a spreadsheet. You need to show the financial benefits, which you can do by measuring things like customer retention, customer referrals, the cost of new customer acquisition, and any other standard matrixes that prove your return on investment. Build out these measurements early on, as you will need to have the data in your quiver at any given time. You never know when an executive will want to see proof that the cool stuff you're doing actually matters.

SHOPPING LIST FOR
CUSTOMER EXPERIENCE SUCCESS

I'd like to leave you with some of my best tips for leading your industry in customer satisfaction, employee engagement, growth, and profit. So here's my short list:

Hire great people—Bad employees bring their badness to work every day. In researching some of the best organizations in the world, I found that they spent an inordinate amount of time focusing on the nature and character of a prospective employee. This is quite different from what most organizations do with a focus on skills, education, and direct experience. Hire employees based on their nature and temperament, and train them to build their skills.

Be the best too—The problem with hiring great people is they expect you to be great too. Bad leaders and bad organizational cultures create organizational antibodies that spit out quality people and that include both customers and team members. Build a mission-centered organization that empowers teams to deliver amazing experiences by giving them the authority to make decisions that serve the customer. *Do good for goodness's sake* because good people want to do good things. Most organizations blame bad customer experiences on frontline stakeholders, when in fact it's customer-punitive policies and destructive cultures that ultimately destroy the customer experience.

Encourage courage—Innovative organizations develop a culture that encourages their teams to take smart risks. The fueling force of innovation is failure. That's right, to develop breakthrough and disruptive innovations that will serve your customer you simply need to be willing to take risks, and that requires business leaders to take the focus off risk and to put it squarely on customer innovation.

Know what your customers crave—Great organizations like Procter & Gamble were pioneers in the concept of touchpoint innovation. Because of their commitment to this approach, they continually develop the best consumer goods in the world. Turns out that all exceptional customer experiences are driven by an organization's understanding of what a customer loves and what they hate across a range of customer types. Some experts suggest that the overwhelming majority of organizations don't really understand what their customers hate and love across a range of experiences. I know I sound redundant, but the headwaters of success are to simply understand what your customers love and hate and then to go about the business of eliminating what they hate while bolstering what they love.

Complete the journey—There's a lot of talk about creating customer journey maps with the idea of developing plans to improve the customer's journey across a range of touchpoints. Unfortunately, most organizations are big on planning and short on deployment. In *What Customers Crave*, I talk about the importance of developing uninterrupted customer experiences across the five customer touchpoints. It is critical that all five touchpoints are exceptional, as most organizations take swipes at this approach and by missing even one experience across the customer's journey they fail as the customer will always remember not the best but rather the worst experience across their journey. Don't just have exceptional experiences at one touchpoint as most organizations do. Deliver exceptional experiences at every touch.

Create the perfect blend—In a world of digital ubiquity, our customers experience us in both physical and digital spaces. Unfortunately, very few organizations deliver exceptional experiences in both digital and non-digital customer environments. The primary reason this happens is that organizations have created departmental silos that rarely result in a blended experience that is communicating the same value, brand promise, and mission in these two environments. Connecting the digital and non-digital worlds in order to deliver an exceptional value to your customer is a requirement in the connected economy.

Develop core competency—In order to win in customer experience and customer service, organizations need to develop customer experience design as a core competency. I believe that begins with getting professional help in designing your customer experience roadmap and in training your executive leadership and team. As conspicuously obvious as this may sound, the organizations that deliver the best customer experiences happen to be extremely competent at customer experience design and deployment.

Be disruptive—The old days of incremental innovation are over, and they're over for good. In a marketplace of hyper competition and rapid technological change, organizations need to go beyond incremental innovations and learn to be market-leading disruptive innovators.

Bring it all together—The problem with leading at innovation and customer experience is that it requires that you build out a functional ecosystem of tools, systems, processes, and technologies. The overwhelming majority of organizations do a fraction of what's required to lead their market. Don't take a swipe at customer experience mastery—bring it all together to create the machinery necessary to predictably deliver the best customer experiences.

TAKEAWAYS

This is going to sound corny, but I am going to say it anyway. Every day we wake up and go to a job, and if it's a job that has a meaningful mission, where we get to make other people happy, we are living a meaningful life. After working with hundreds of companies over the years, I have seen beautiful people destroy their lives by working in organizations that mistreat their customers. Customer experience is more than just treating customers well. It's about architecting a machine that serves others.

And isn't that what we're here for: to serve others, to live a life of meaning, and to make people happy? The most successful people I've ever met would quickly answer that question with an emphatic, "Hell yes!"

END NOTES

CHAPTER 1

1. "New Oracle Global Research Study Finds That Brands Could Lose Up to 20% of Revenue Due to Poor Customer Experiences, Yet Many Struggle to Develop Successful Strategies," www.oracle.com/us/corporate/press /1903222.

2. Help Scout, "75 Customer Service Facts, Quotes & Statistics: How Your Business Can Deliver with the Best of the Best," www.helpscout.net/75 -customer-service-facts-quotes-statistics/.

3. "Mobile Search Moments: Understanding How Mobile Drives Conversions," Life360 Presentation, March 2013, ssl.gstatic.com/think/docs /creating-moments-that-matter_research-studies.pdf.

4. "Micro-Moments," *Think with Google* (blog), www.thinkwithgoogle.com /collections/micromoments.html.

5. "Cooks Make Tastier Food When They Can See Their Customers," *Harvard Business Review*, November 2014, hbr.org/2014/11/cooks-make -tastier-food-when-they-can-see-their-customers.

CHAPTER 3

1. Ruby Newell-Legner, "Understanding Customers," cited in 75 Customer Service Facts, Quotes & Statistics: How Your Business Can Deliver with the Best of the Best, www.helpscout.net/75-customer-service-facts -quotes-statistics/.

2. American Express Survey, 2011, cited in 75 Customer Service Facts.

3. Henrik Bresman, "What Millennials Want from Work, Charted Across the World," *Harvard Business Review*, February 23, 2015, hbr.org/2015/02 /what-millennials-want-from-work-charted-across-the-world.

4. White House Office of Consumer Affairs, cited in 75 Customer Service Facts.

5. Ibid.

6. Marketing Metrics, cited in 75 Customer Service Facts.

CHAPTER 7

1. "Zero Moment of Truth (ZMOT)," *Think with Google* (blog), www .thinkwithgoogle.com/collections/zero-moment-truth.html.

CHAPTER 11

1. Aaron E. Carroll, "To Be Sued Less, Doctors Should Consider Talking to Patients More," *New York Times*, June 1, 2015, www.nytimes.com/2015 /06/02/upshot/to-be-sued-less-doctors-should-talk-to-patients-more .html?_r=0.

INDEX

CONTACT THE AUTHOR

Nick is always excited to learn about how his readers have applied his methods to drive world-class customer experiences in their own organizations. He can be contacted through his consulting and training firm at www.mylearnlogic.com or for speaking engagements at www.nickwebb.com.

ABOUT THE AUTHOR

Nick Webb is one of the top customer experience and customer service experts in the world. He has been awarded the Global Gurus Top 30 designation for customer service for seven years in a row. Nick is the CEO of goLeaderLogic.com, a customer experience training and advisory firm that works with some of the top brands to help them build world-class customer experiences.

As a technologist, he has been awarded more than forty US patents for consumer and technology products.

Nick is the author of multiple number one bestselling books in the areas of business innovation, customer experience, and leadership. He is also one of the top keynote speakers in the areas of business growth, innovation, future trends, and customer experience.